THE COMPLETE SEAFOOD BOOK

THE COMPLETE SEAFOOD BOOK

JAMES WAGENVOORD AND WOODMAN HARRIS

MACMILLAN PUBLISHING COMPANY

NEW YORK

COLLIER MACMILLAN PUBLISHERS

LONDON

A JAMES WAGENVOORD STUDIO, INC. BOOK

EDITOR
James Wagenvoord

ASSOCIATE EDITOR
Patricia Coen

WRITERS
James Wagenvoord
Patricia Coen
Woodman Harris

ASSISTANT EDITOR
Faith S. Brown

DESIGN
Nancy L. Talmadge

ARTIST-ILLUSTRATOR
Karen Rolnick

COPY EDITOR
Amy Lipton

EDITORIAL ASSISTANTS
Judith Hill
Annick Oczkowski

ART ASSISTANTS
Lydia Hidalgo   Robert Taylor
Rhoda Leichter   Keren Dick

Macmillan Publishing Company
866 Third Avenue, New York, N.Y. 10022
Collier Macmillan Canada, Inc.

Library of Congress Catalog Card Number: 83-17551

10 9 8 7 6 5 4 3 2 1

Printed in the United States of America

ACKNOWLEDGMENTS

We would like to thank the many people who gave us their time and insight during the creation of this book:

Fiona St. Aubyn, Harold Coren, Jimmy Schmidt, Patrick Terrail, John Grisanti, David Gooch, Elliot Baron, Andrew Silverman, Cathi Nye, William and Juanita Coen, Ralph Parden, Craig Ghio, Bobi Moses, Barbara Chapin, Penny Shiroma, Carol Rose Rose, Susan Chicoine, Lisa Stern, Patti Tucci, John Munson, Pasquale Coli, Sam Chownwai, Roger Berkowitz, Brian Halloran, Steve Buich, Joan Perlof, John Canepa, Kathy Pohl, David Quinn, Woolley Beresford, Carole Brown, Herbert B. Story, Jr., Roy Hymen, Harvey Riezenman, Samuel Bookbinder, Richard Bookbinder, Claire Johnson, David C. Wilson, Mike Neely, Michael O'Neal, Cecilia Decastro, William F. Gusey, Susan Laufer, Terrance R. Leary, Maggie Horne, Mary M. Habeson, Karen Fourhaltz, Sam Yeung, David Ferelli, Wendy Sewall, Irene D. Huff, Yvonne Boyer, David H. G. Gould, Kittie Kuhns, Lilian Lorenzsonn-Willis, Michael Allsup, Toby A. Redmond, Francis Scarano, Bertha Fontaine, Betty E. Tuhkunen, Robert M. Beaudoin, Lila Goldin, Jerry Sarnat, Diane Chavan, Keren Dick, Roger Rouillier and Joseph Cornacchia.

The following organizations provided valuable information and assistance: Sea Grant, Maine's Department of Marine Resources, Gulf of Mexico Fishery Management Council, United States Department of Commerce, United States Department of the Interior, Fisheries Communications, Inc., National Oceanic and Atmospheric Administration, South Atlantic Fishery Management Council, North Carolina Wildlife Resources Commission, New Jersey Marine Advisory Service, Department of Environmental Conservation, Fishing News Books, Ltd., Duke University Marine Laboratory, United Nations Division of Food and Agriculture, Scripps Institute of Oceanography, Seafood Business Report, Mid-Atlantic Fisheries Development Foundation, Maryland Waterman's Association, National Marine Fisheries Service, Alabama Cooperative Extension Service and West Coast Fisheries Development Foundation.

CONTENTS

THE GIFT OF THE SEAS

Commercial fishing, one of the nation's oldest industries, is in the midst of a renaissance after languishing for most of this century in the shadow of the American red meat feast, which is only now waning. Today there is a growing national tendency to avoid chemical food additives and eat less processed food and more fresh food, particularly vegetables, fruits and seafood.

The early signals of an increased interest in seafood came from the restaurant industry

continued

where, in 1978, seafood became the No. 1 entree. Today it continues to grow in popularity.

THE BUSINESS OF SEAFOOD

Throughout history, fish and shellfish have been a vital part of the human diet. When people first began to fish, they were attracted to food from the sea because of its accessibility and flavor. Fish was abundant and, in many instances, easier to catch and kill than large land animals. Prehistoric man caught fish by hand from streams. During the Stone Age, man developed crude hooks, nets and traps to capture shallow-water fish. Hundreds of years before Christ, the Chinese spun silk fishing lines; the Egyptians wove twine made from flax into sturdy nets for gathering fish; the ancient Greeks built traps designed to capture tuna traveling through the Mediterranean past the shores of Greece. And as early as the fifth century B.C., people realized that fish, like any other crop, could be farmed. They dug ponds and stocked them with fish for personal consumption and for trade. (This practice continues in parts of the United States today.) Eventually, the lure of larger fish in deeper waters prompted fishermen to build ocean-going vessels and more advanced equipment.

Recreational fishing, unlike most other forms of hunting, can be as relaxing or challenging as the fisherman cares to make it. He can sit on a bank near a quiet stream with a simple pole and line, catching fish that swim by and preparing them for his dinner. Or, he can go out to sea in a large sports-fishing boat and, using more elaborate equipment, attempt to hook and do battle with large game fish.

Commercial fishing, however, has been vital to the United States since the eighteenth century, when the early colonists depended upon the sea as a major food source. The American fishing industry has developed and grown since the days when fishermen in schooners sailed the seas month after month in search of fish. Today fishermen use sophisticated vessels equipped with electronic gear and radar, often in conjunction with helicopters, to locate large schools of fish.

Despite the significance that fish have had in our culture, their nutritional qualities were not always fully recognized. America began its addiction to red meat in the nineteenth century, and fish and shellfish took second place behind beef, pork and poultry.

In the health-conscious eighties, however, Americans became more aware of the importance of sound nutrition, of

lowering calorie and cholesterol intake and consuming an adequate amount of vitamins, proteins and minerals. Seafood has
taken on renewed significance.

SEAFOOD COAST TO COAST

Today, coordination among fisherman, distributors, airlines,
wholesalers and retailers is common, resulting in a wide
variety of fresh seafood available from coast to coast. It is common to see Alaska salmon from the Bering Sea, for example, in
restaurants and supermarkets throughout the country within
48 hours of being caught.

Retailers are participating in the air shipping of seafood
because they recognize an increased demand for fresh seafood.
Most major supermarket chains are paying more attention to
seafood, and seafood departments staffed by carefully trained
personnel are opening within markets throughout the country
at the rate of more 1,500 each year. Government agencies are
working to improve the quality of seafood in the sea and on the
dock, as well as during processing and transporting.

SEAFOOD FOR HEALTH

Unlike other high-protein foods including beef, there are
well over 100 varieties of fish and shellfish commercially available to choose from, each with its own flavor subtleties and
characteristics. Many people are concerned about the calories
they consume and, although the fat content of fish varies from
species to species, most fish have a low fat content, making
them ideal for weight-reducing diets. Even those fish higher in
fat are healthful—the fat they contain is composed primarily of
polyunsaturated fatty acids and may actually help to dis-
courage cholesterol from building up in the veins and arteries.

Because seafood is highly digestible, it is particularly good
for children, the elderly, and anyone with digestive problems.
Fish and shellfish are an excellent source of dietary essentials,
and its cost per pound is no higher—and is often lower—than
that of most land animals. Seafood plays a vital role in the
development of a balanced diet.

PROTEIN

Fish and shellfish contain a high proportion of protein rich in
the amino acids needed to repair and generate body tissue.

Four ounces of most types of fish will supply about half the total amount of protein required by the body each day. And fish protein, from either lean or fatty fish, is 85 to 95 percent digestible, which insures that the body will use it efficiently.

FAT

Although there is no conclusive evidence, medical research indicates that consumption of fat containing polyunsaturated fatty acids tends to lower blood cholesterol levels. The body does need saturated fats and cholesterol, but only in limited quantities. It is difficult, however, to control the intake of these elements. Beef is high in saturated fats; seafood contains the needed unsaturated fats and small amounts of cholesterol.

CALORIES

Reducing one's calorie intake is often as important as including liberal amounts of polyunsaturated fats to insure a balanced diet. Served as a low-calorie entree, seafood provides adequate protein to meet the body's needs. Low-fat fish and shellfish normally contain fewer than 100 calories per 4-ounce serving, while a 4-ounce serving of beef may supply well over 300 calories. Incorporating seafood into a weight-reduction diet has a distinct advantage over eating foods that are high in fat. The high protein content of seafood is complemented by the low calorie count, providing a nutritional bargain for the consumer.

VITAMINS AND MINERALS

Seafoods are supplementary vitamin lenders. Certain fatty fish are good sources of vitamin D and many lean fish supply adequate amounts of B vitamins. (The B-vitamin content of fish is about the same as that of land animals.)

Fish also contain large amounts of phosphorous, potassium and iron. Even saltwater species are relatively low in sodium and can often be used in low-salt diets. Fresh oysters and soft clams are low in sodium, but some other shellfish contain higher salt levels.

Seafood is also noted for its valuable trace minerals, including iodine, fluorine and selenium. One recent study indicates that selenium has anticarcinogenic properties. This study indicates that cancer in mice can be prevented by feeding the animals a diet supplemented by selenium. Seafood is the richest natural source of selenium. Most essential trace minerals are present in seafoods in amounts at least equivalent to those found in meat, and usually in greater quantities than those found in vegetables and dairy products.

BETTER EATING

In addition to their healthful qualities, fish and shellfish contribute to the enjoyment of eating. Over 100 varieties, both fresh and processed, are available. With this variety of choice you can find seafood to suit even the most discriminating palate. Seafood, however, is extremely delicate and must be handled with care, whether it is fresh or frozen. Its natural nutrients and taste can be diminished through improper processing and preservation techniques. Unlike many types of beef, which tends to improve with age, fish and shellfish are at their best when eaten fresh or fresh-frozen.

Until the twentieth century, fresh fish and shellfish were available only to those who lived near the shore. But today, swift transportation methods have made seafood available to everyone, regardless of their distance from the sea. And, since preservation techniques have been perfected, fish stays "fresh-caught" much longer than it used to.

To maintain that fresh flavor, the methods used to cook seafood are just as important as processing and preservation techniques. Fish needs to be properly cooked to bring out its full flavor. Fish should be cooked only until the flesh "sets" and can be easily flaked from the bones. Although seafood needs to be handled with care, it isn't difficult to prepare. The simplest cooking methods are often the best. Remember that fish and shellfish are a truly enjoyable dining experience.

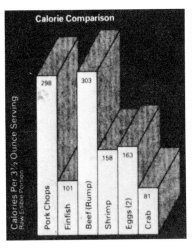
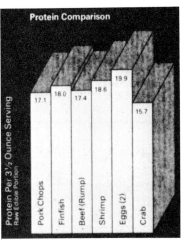

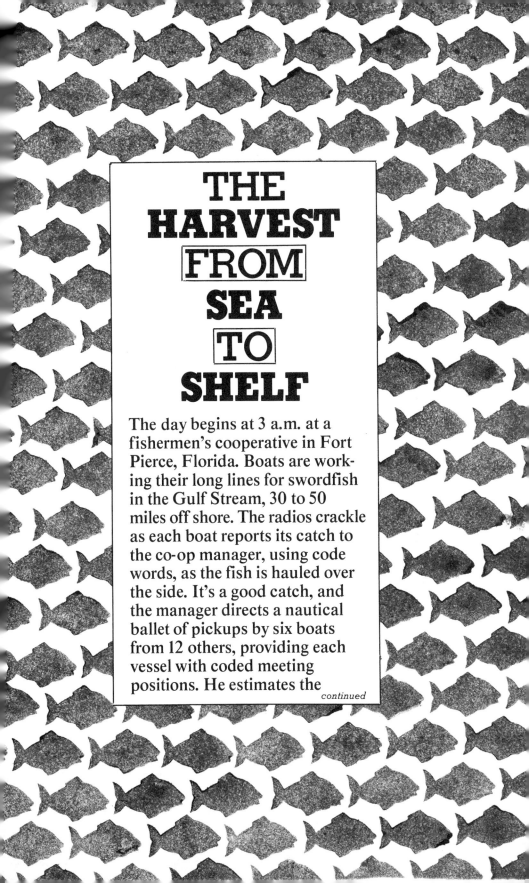

THE HARVEST FROM SEA TO SHELF

The day begins at 3 a.m. at a
fishermen's cooperative in Fort
Pierce, Florida. Boats are working their long lines for swordfish
in the Gulf Stream, 30 to 50
miles off shore. The radios crackle
as each boat reports its catch to
the co-op manager, using code
words, as the fish is hauled over
the side. It's a good catch, and
the manager directs a nautical
ballet of pickups by six boats
from 12 others, providing each
vessel with coded meeting
positions. He estimates the

continued

arrival time, and dispatches a truck to Orlando to pick up large containers from two major airlines, reserving space at the same time for morning flights to Boston, New York, Chicago, Houston, Denver and Los Angeles.

The large fish are bled, headed, gutted and iced en route, and by 5:30 a.m. a dozen workers have begun to move the fish off the boats, put them through a brief cleansing, trimming and packaging process, and place them in the air containers. Back in Orlando by 8:30 a.m., the containers are loaded aboard the planes within minutes of departure, and arrive at their destination airports by noon. During the morning, tallies of the fish by size, weight, and color have been communicated to stores and restaurants in cities nationwide. Deliveries are made directly from the airports, and fish are served for dinner, thousands of miles from Fort Pierce, the same day they are caught.

Although this scenario takes place in the Gulf, it occurs in other major ports as well—Boston and Gloucester, Massachusetts; Hampton and Norfolk, Virginia; Kodiak and Dutch Harbor, Alaska; San Pedro and San Diego, California; Key West, Florida; Biloxi, Mississippi; and Brownsville and Port Isabel, Texas. The process the fish undergoes between the time it is caught and the time it is sold to a retailer or restaurant is a fast but complicated one.

THE COMMERCIAL CHAIN

Fishing boats receive one daily price for each type of fish they catch. Each boat must deduct from its profit the expenses of unloading, icing and boxing the fish, which run between seven cents and 10 cents per pound. If a boat is paid 30 cents per pound for a particular (relatively inexpensive) fish, it will net only about 22 cents per pound. The primary dealer who purchased the fish at 30 cents may sell some of the fish to other dealers, whom he will typically charge five cents over his cost or, in this case 35 cents per pound. If the fish is to processed, as most fish are, the buyer must pay the cost of transporting the fish to the processing plant—usually about five cents per pound; the cost of cutting the fish into fillets is about 10 cents per pound, packaging costs are about seven cents per pound, and the additional cost of transporting the fish from the plant to a regional marketplace is about another five cents per pound.

If a whole fish is cut into fillets, its weight is decreased by about two thirds—a commercial buyer who pays for a three-pound fish may end up with only a one-pound fillet to sell. If the fish is airfreighted to a regional marketplace, as many fish are, there's usually a charge of 20 cents to 50 cents per pound for shipping and handling. In the marketplace, the fish will be marked up by 10 to 15 percent; the wholesaler who buys the fish will add about 15 percent to the price he pays, and the retailer who buys it from him will mark it up an additional 35 percent when he sells it to you. A pound of fish that earned the fisherman 22 cents may cost you between $1.10 and $1.60, depending on the origin of the fish and the number of middlemen involved. In the case of rare or out-of-season fish the dockside cost is generally higher, as is the final price, but the average percentage markups remain fairly consistent.

MAKING THE CATCH

Sports and commercial fisherman use a variety of techniques to catch fish—there really aren't any hard and fast rules. The methods depend on the species of fish they're seeking, the depth of the water in which the fish live, the type of boat and equipment available and the fisherman's personal preferences. What follows are some of the most commonly used methods of catching fish.

LINES AND TECHNIQUES

An individual fisherman, using a pole and line, may practice *bottom fishing*, a technique in which the line is weighted so the bait rests on or near the bottom. This is practiced on bottom-dwelling fish, primarily flounder. To catch fish nearer the surface, the fisherman may *live line*, or allow a natural bait, live or dead, to drift in the current or be suspended by a float. To attract fish to the vicinity of a boat, fishermen often *chum*, a technique in which bait is scattered along the surface of the water. Sometimes fish are more attracted to bait that moves and appears to be alive, and in these cases a fisherman might *troll*, or trail a baited line behind a slowly moving boat. He might also *cast*, a technique in which he throws out bait attached to a hook and line, allowing it to strike the water so that it can be pulled back rapidly or allowed to drift with the current.

Large commercial vessels use variations of these techniques, as well as some that are more efficient. A *long line* is a line several miles long that has buoys and as many as 1,500 hooks attached to it at fixed intervals. The line is left in the water for several hours, then hauled in with fish attached. Most swordfish are caught with this technique, as are some tuna.

THE NETS

GILL NET

OTTER TRAWL

FISH TRAPPED IN SEINE NET

PURSE SEINE

Professional fishermen tend to rely more on nets than on lines, since they can usually harvest a greater number of fish with nets. The *gill net* is used in relatively shallow water to capture fish known to be in certain areas at certain times, including salmon heading toward rivers and schools of fish that pass the same coastline at about the same time every year. The gill net has openings that are large enough to allow small fish to pass through unharmed, while the fish that the net is designed to catch can pass through only as far as their gills. When the fish realizes it can't go forward it tries to back out and its gills become entangled. The fish remains trapped until the net is hauled in to collect the catch.

The *otter trawl*, a cone-shaped, completely enclosed net with a wide mouth, is an effective device used to catch fish that live near the bottom. The trawl is dragged along the bottom behind a boat, and fish are swept into the wide opening. They are swept further back into the narrower portion of the net as it is dragged. The word *trawl* refers simply to a net that is pulled behind a moving boat, and can refer to many different types of nets.

A *seine* net is one with smaller mesh, designed to enclose fish within it rather than trap them in the mesh, as in the case of the gill net. The size of the holes in the mesh vary according to the fish the net is designed to trap. The *haul seine* is a net that's stretched from the beach to a buoy anchored offshore. Fish swimming near it are trapped as it is hauled in an arc back to shore. A *stop seine* is a small net that can be thrown over a group of fish. It lays flat on the water, but weights and sinkers around its perimeter drag its ends down slightly, encircling the fish over which it floats. It can be pulled closed with a draw-string and hauled in by the fisherman. The *purse seine*, used by commercial fishermen to harvest schools of large fish, is a cir-cular net that hangs in the water like a cylinder. A drawstring pulls the bottom shut, and although the top remains open near the surface, fish are trapped within it. The purse seine became important to the commercial fishing industry after World War II, when a hydraulic device capable of pulling the large, heavy net up into a boat was developed.

CATCHING SHELLFISH

There is also a variety of methods used to catch shellfish. Crabs are often caught commercially with *trot lines*, ropes that are approximately a quarter of a mile to one mile long, with a buoy on one end and a chain anchor on the other. Crabs grasp the bait and simply hold on to the line. Fishermen check the line periodically and gather the crabs. Crabs are also caught in *crab pots*, wire boxes approximately two feet square. Each box has two chambers, the bottom one baited. The crab enters the bottom chamber, takes the bait and begins to swim upward, becoming trapped in the upper chamber. A similar system is used to catch lobsters. A *lobster pot* is an oblong box made of wooden planks spaced far enough apart to allow small lobsters to escape. The ends of the pots are covered with funnel-shaped netting which makes escape difficult.

CRAB POT

LOBSTER POT

FREQUENTLY ASKED QUESTIONS ABOUT SEAFOOD

Q: *WHERE DOES SEAFOOD COME FROM?*

A: The United States exports one third of the seafood we catch, and imports more than half of the seafood we eat. We export salmon, herring, king and snow crab, squid and processed shrimp, in large quantities primarily to Canada, France, The United Kingdom and Venezuela. We import large quantities of shrimp, tuna and groundfish fillets and blocks primarily from Canada, Japan and Iceland. Seafood is the third largest category of negative trade balance, after oil and automobiles. Increasing quantities of fresh groundfish are being imported from Canada and Iceland, and farmed salmon is being imported from Norway and Denmark.

Q: *IS SEAFOOD GOVERNMENT GRADED THE SAME WAY MEAT IS?*

A: There is a voluntary government inspection program available to processors of prepackaged or "tray pack" seafood, but most fresh fish is still packed bulk, and most seafood plants are not government inspected. Your best assurance of quality is the knowledge and integrity of your seafood retailer.

GLOSSARY

BASTE: *Moisten by spooning a liquid over a roast or other food as it cooks.*

BATTER: *A mixture of flour and a liquid, which is thin enough to pour.*

BEAT: *Make a mixture smooth by a vigorous over-and-over motion with a spoon.*

BIND: *Add a liquid, egg or melted fat to a dry mixture to hold it together.*

BLANCH: *Dip in and out of boiling water to loosen the skins of fruits or vegetables.*

BLEND: *Combine ingredients thoroughly until very smooth and uniform.*

BOIL: *Heat until bubbles rise continuously and break on the surface of the liquid* (**ROLLING BOIL**: *bubbles form rapidly*).

BRAISE: *Cook tightly covered in a small amount of liquid at a low temperature, either in the oven or over direct heat. When braising meat, brown it in fat before adding the liquid.*

BROWN: *Cook until food changes color, usually in a small amount of fat over moderate heat.*

Q: WHAT ARE THE 10 MOST POPULAR SEAFOOD SPECIES?

A: Salmon, tuna, shrimp, crab, pollock, flounder, cod, herring, hake and mackerel.

Q: IS THERE A BEST DAY OF THE WEEK TO BUY FISH?

A: Seafood has become more popular for weekend eating in recent years, both in restaurants and at home. Most restaurants, supermarkets and fish stores buy their heaviest supplies on Thursday, Friday and Monday. With overnight delivery by truck and air commonplace, fresh high-quality seafood is available every day.

Q: WHAT ARE THE LEAST EXPENSIVE SEAFOODS TO EAT?

A: Mussels, squid, pollock, mackerel, whiting, butterfish and cod are usually less expensive than the more popular fish such as flounder, sole and salmon. They are every bit as nutritious, and recipes abound for them all.

Q: WHICH IS THE BETTER BUY—WHOLE FISH OR FILLETS?

A: Whole fish are generally less expensive than fillets, but you should be aware of the yield as an offsetting factor. Most groundfish yield between 25 and 40 percent of their whole weight. If both forms are available, ask your retailer what the yield factor is, and calculate the best buy yourself.

Q: ARE THERE LESS COSTLY WAYS OF SERVING SEAFOOD?

A: Individual fillets, steaks or lobsters are not your only choices. Any of the fresher fish may be poached, broken up and used as a highly nutritious base for casseroles and soups that use other foods as stretchers. Look for the advertised "in season" specials, buy in quantity and freeze. Try the underutilized species—butterfish, squid, ocean perch and whiting, for example—for which demand is not great and bargains are often available. Remember that pound for pound seafood is more nutritious than beef, pork and poultry.

Q: WHERE SHOULD I BUY SEAFOOD—IN A SEAFOOD STORE OR A SUPERMARKET?

A: You should buy seafood from a reputable source—either an independent store or a supermarket. The more knowledgeable you are, the easier it is for you to judge the quality of the seafood for sale. Don't be afraid to ask questions—a good retailer will be willing and able to answer them. Remember, high price does not necessarily insure good quality nor does low price mean poor quality.

Q: HOW SHOULD I STORE FRESH FISH UNTIL I USE IT?

A: The most important thing is to remove seafood from its butcher-wrap type covering, if purchased from a seafood retailer, or from the tray pack if purchased from a self-service department. Rewrap it in a freezer paper that will hold moisture. Fresh seafood that has not been used within two days should be frozen.

Q: HOW MUCH DO I NEED TO BUY?

A: If you're buying whole fish, you should purchase approximately one pound per person. Bone-in steaks require 10 to 12 ounces per person. Boneless fillets require six to nine ounces, depending on appetite. One and one-quarter pound lobsters are large enough to satisfy most people, as are six cooked shrimp for shrimp cocktails. Six is also a good number for little necks, cherrystones, oysters, sea scallops and smelts. One dozen mussels or bay scallops are generally enough to satisfy, as are four to six cooked blue crabs or two good-sized soft shell crabs.

Q: AM I GETTING GOOD NUTRITIONAL VALUE FOR MY DOLLARS WHEN I BUY SEAFOOD?

A: Yes. As the medical profession continues to become more knowledgeable about human nutrition, seafood receives more attention for its contributions to health maintenance and healing. There is a positive correlation between seafood consumption and improved cardiovascular efficiency, i.e., limiting the build-up of plaque, hardened fats and/or cholesterol that line the walls of arteries and veins.

Q: HOW OFTEN SHOULD I EAT SEAFOOD?

A: Most nutritionists counsel that a balanced diet is best. With so many Americans becoming more aware of nutrition and *unhealthy* foods, people are seeking out higher quality fresh food in fruits, vegetables and seafood, and avoiding foods processed with sugar, sodium, fats and breading. We recommend seafood, preferably fresh, at least three times a week.

GLOSSARY

CHOP: *Cut into pieces with a knife or other sharp tool (hold knife tip on the board with one hand; move the blade up and down with the other).*

CLARIFIED BUTTER: *Butter that has been melted, allowed to stand, and had the fat skimmed from the top.*

COAT: *Cover food to be fried with batter of flour, egg and bread crumbs; cover food that is cooked or ready to serve with a thin layer of mayonnaise or sauce.*

COOK AND STIR: *Cook food in a small amount of shortening until tender, stirring occasionally.*

COOL: *Allow to come to room temperature.*

CREAM: *Beat just until smooth, light and fluffy; the combination of sugar and shortening.*

CREAM: *Beat together fat and sugar to resemble whipped cream in color and texture—pale and fluffy. This method of mixing is used for cakes and puddings containing a high proportion of fat.*

CRUSH: *Press to extract juice with side of knife (garlic).*

GLOSSARY

CUBE: *Cut into cubes ½-inch or larger.*

DEEP FAT FRYING (FRENCH FRYING): *Heat fat at least 1 inch deep in pan with sides at least 5 inches deep.*

DICE: *Cut into small cubes less than ½-inch.*

DOUBLE BOILER: *A pan consisting of a bottom pot to hold boiling water and a top pot in which food is placed. The food is heated by the steam from the boiling water.*

DREDGE: *Coat with flour or sugar.*

DUST: *Sprinkle lightly with flour or sugar.*

GLAZE: *Cover with a transparent coating of jelly, meat juices or caramel.*

GRATE: *Cut into tiny particles using the small holes of a grater.*

GRILL: *Cook food by direct heat under a broiler or grill or over a hot fire.*

JULIENNE: *Cut into match-like sticks.*

KNEAD: *Work a dough firmly, using the knuckles for bread-making and the finger-tips for pastry-making. In both cases the outside of the dough is drawn into the center.*

Q: HOW DO CHEMICALS AND POLLUTION IN THE WATER AFFECT SEAFOOD?

A: Food poisoning from uncooked seafood is a remote but real possibility. We suggest you steer clear of seafood in the raw. There is so much variety in species and cooking methods that you'll never lack a new dish to try. Most potentially harmful forms of water pollution, chemicals and parasites are either exposed or neutralized in cooking. If you must have your shellfish raw, inspect it carefully before eating. Turn clam and oyster meat over and look for off-color, particularly a dull or milky excess, and off-odor. To our knowledge, there has never been a case of mercury poisoning from swordfish in this country. If you want to be ultra-cautious, get your swordfish steaks from fish weighing less than 150 pounds.

Q: WHY IS CATFISH GAINING IN POPULARITY?

A: Catfish farming has become a sizable industry in the United States. Only 15 years old, the catfish industry now produces more than 100 million pounds, or better than 3 percent of our entire edible seafood supply. Catfish convert their food weight into body weight at a ratio of 1.25 to 1, higher than any other farmed product, including beef cattle, hogs and chickens. This fact, coupled with a higher dollar-per-acre yield than rice, has caused many farmers to convert rice acreage to ponds for raising catfish. A leading national supermarket chain now owns its own catfish farms, and has promoted this species into its second best-selling species out of more than 50 species carried during a year.

Q: WHAT IS RED TIDE?

A: Red tide is an algae bloom, the spectacular growth of something called single-cell dinoflagellates, that multiply geometrically in the time it takes to blink. While not themselves toxic to other marine species, they can rapidly deplete the water's oxygen supply and suffocate many species of fish. They are toxic to humans, so accidental consumption of shellfish from a red tide infested area can cause serious illness.

Q: WHY ARE SEAFOOD PRICES SO VOLATILE?

A: Fresh seafood prices are considerably more volatile than those of frozen seafood because of the unpredictable nature of fishing. Prices are lower when a species is in season, which means it is available more readily and easier to catch.

Q: DOES FISH CONTAIN FEWER PRESERVATIVES THAN MEAT?

A: Yes. Fillet plants use chlorinated water, similar to that used in swimming pools, to keep naturally occurring algae and bacteria counts down. Some processors use a light saltwater rinse to keep moisture on the surface of their product. You should rinse this off in fresh water before cooking. Some frozen fish is dipped in sodiumtripolyphosphate to retain internal moisture throughout freezing and storage life. There are none of the other added vitamins, hormones, minerals or dyes in fresh seafood that are commonly used in beef, pork and poultry.

Q: HOW MUCH DOES FISH SHRINK IN COOKING?

A: Most fish shrinks between 10 and 15 percent, about 35 percent from shell-on to cooked, cleaned shrimp.

Q: DO FISH FILLETS TASTE BETTER IF COOKED WITH THE SKIN ON?

A: Slightly more liquid is retained by cooking with the skin on, so slightly more of the natural flavor remains.

Q: WHAT ABOUT THE BONES?

A: If you are purchasing fillets, ask your fishmonger to remove the bones, particularly the pin bone at the front or thick end of the fillet. Almost all whole, cooked fish can be deboned at the table by removing the top fillet and simply lifting up the "rack" of spine and ribs. Do this from head to tail, so as not to snap some ribs and leave them behind. This will not work with shad, bonito or crevalle jacks, which have more complicated skeletons.

Q: IS IT POSSIBLE TO BECOME ILL FROM EATING SEAFOOD?

A: Yes. We do not recommend eating raw seafood, particularly shellfish. There have been cases of food poisoning due to polluted water harvesting, which is illegal. Shellfish grounds, particularly clam and oyster beds, are checked regularly by state officials for wholesomeness, and all clams, oysters and mussels traveling through interstate commerce are tagged and traceable from the retailer all the way back to the harvester.

GLOSSARY

LUKEWARM: *Moderately warm; approximately 100° F.*

MARINATE: *Cover with a liquid and let stand to season or to become tender.*

MINCE: *Cut into very small pieces.*

PAN-BOIL: *Cook in a shallow, heavy pan over direct heat.*

PAN-FRY: *Heat cooking oil or fat in a frying pan large enough to hold the food in a single layer.*

PARBOIL: *Cook partially in preparation for further cooking.*

PARE: *Cut off outer covering with a knife or other sharp tool.*

PEEL: *Strip off outer covering.*

POACH: *Cook in an open pan at simmering point, with liquid sufficiently seasoned to cover.*

REDUCE: *Cook a liquid until some has been carried off as steam.*

REDUCE: *Boil a liquid (especially when making a soup, sauce or syrup) in an uncovered pan to evaporate surplus liquid and provide a more concentrated result.*

23

Q: HAS THAT SHRIMP BEEN FROZEN?

A: The answer most of the time is yes. There are times throughout the year when fresh shrimp is available but the supply is not nearly enough to meet the demand. Most shrimp is imported and has been frozen. Your retailer thaws it as a convenience to you.

Q: WHY IS COOKED AND CLEANED SHRIMP SO EXPENSIVE?

A: Shrimp loses weight in cooking as well as in cleaning and deveining. Your retailer's prices reflect the fact that the pound of shrimp he purchased is less than a pound after he cleans it. For the most part, the same methods of catching shrimp have been employed for many years and productivity has not kept pace with demand. For years the primary source of shrimp has been the Gulf of Mexico and the Caribbean. The price may stabilize as more high-quality shrimp are imported from Asia and as shrimp farming becomes commercially feasible.

Q: WHAT IS THE BEST WAY TO CLEAN WHOLE SHRIMP?

A: Shrimp are easier to clean after cooking. Add a tablespoon of salad oil to the boiling water. This loosens the shell, which can then be peeled just as you would peel the shell of a hard-boiled egg. A lengthwise cut down the middle of the outside of the curled shrimp will expose the intestinal tract, which should be rinsed clean. Cooked shrimp should be chilled immediately after cleaning, and may be stored several hours or overnight in ice cold water. Squeeze a lemon or lime into the water half an hour before serving.

Q: DO SMALLER SHRIMP TASTE AS GOOD AS LARGER ONES?

A: Yes, but they are a little more difficult to clean. Also, you must be especially careful not to overcook small shrimp, as they will toughen quickly.

Q: WHAT IS THE BEST WAY TO COOK LOBSTER?

A: There is no best method. The most popular methods are boiling, broiling, steaming and baking. Be careful not to let the meat dry out when broiling a split lobster. We prefer steaming to boiling, since steaming locks in the juices and doesn't dilute the flavor with excess liquid. If you're squeamish about cooking a live lobster, ask your retailer to cook it for you. Most retailers have cooking facilities.

Q: HOW CAN I KEEP A LOBSTER ALIVE AT HOME?

A: *DO NOT* run a cold tub for it! Fresh water quickly kills a lobster. For up to 36 hours out of water, lobsters need a dark, cold, wet environment with oxygen readily available. We recommend a drawer in your refrigerator. Cover it with seaweed if available, or wet newspaper.

Q: WHERE DO FROZEN LOBSTER TAILS COME FROM?

A: Almost no North Atlantic lobsters are processed for lobster tails. Virtually all lobster tails consumed come from one of several species of rock lobster. Australia, New Zealand and South Africa all produce high-quality tails from cold-water rock lobsters, while Brazil, most Central American countries, the Bahamas and Florida produce warm-water spiny-rock lobster tails. Generally speaking, cold-water tails taste sweeter.

Q: WHAT ARE CHIX? WHAT IS A CULL?

A: Chix are minimum legal-sized lobsters, weighing between 15 ounces and one and one quarter pounds. Lobsters are measured by fishermen with a metal gauge that reads carapace length from eye socket to tail joint. This measurement must be 3 3/16-inches long to be a keeper; shorter lobsters must be returned to the sea. A cull is a one-clawed lobster, usually the victim of some previous combat. Culls are usually cheaper, and yield more tail meat per pound.

Q: ARE OYSTERS REALLY ONLY GOOD DURING THE MONTHS ENDING IN "R"?

A: This is one of the great old myths. Oysters are available year round. We recommend buying oyster meats instead of oysters in the shell for the following reasons:

a. You don't have to shuck and clean oyster meats.
b. They're often cheaper than oysters in the shell.
c. Opened oysters are graded by size, so you can expect more consistent size.
d. There's no loss from the occasional mudder or empty shell, or oysters shrunken from the energy expended on spawning.

Q: CAN I FREEZE OYSTERS, CLAMS AND MUSSELS?

A: Yes, and you can expect the shells to open easily upon thawing.

GLOSSARY

SLIVER: *Cut into long, thin pieces.*

SNIP: *Cut into very small pieces with scissors.*

SPONGE: *A batter to which yeast has been added.*

STEEP: *Pour hot or cold water over food and leave it to stand, to soften it or extract its flavor and color (tea).*

STERILIZE: *Boil for 20 minutes.*

STEW: *Cook in liquid deep enough to cover.*

STOCK: *The liquid produced when meat, bones, poultry, fish or vegetables are simmered in water with herbs and flavorings for several hours to extract their flavor.*

THICKEN: *Give body to soups, sauces or gravies by adding flour, cornstarch or arrowroot.*

TOAST: *Brown in oven or toaster.*

WHIP: *Beat rapidly to incorporate air.*

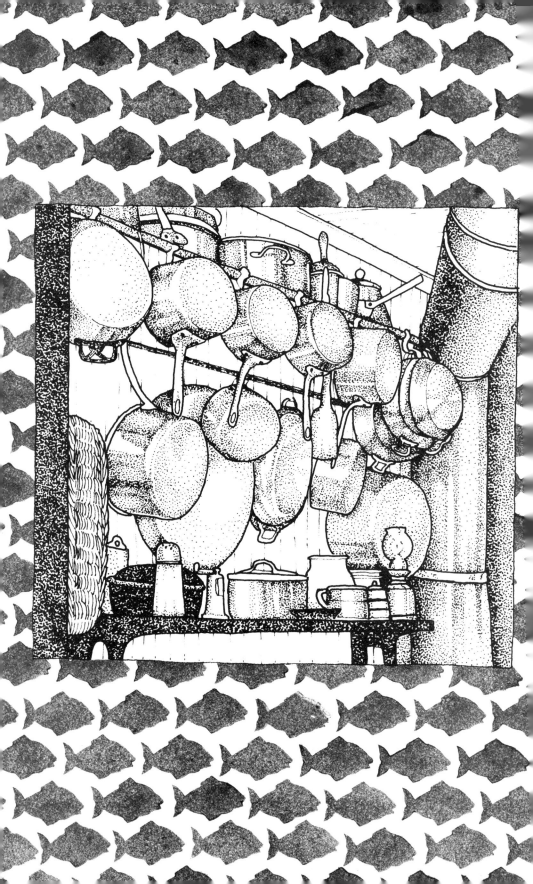

SEA FOOD COOKERY

Fish and shellfish are often called "Nature's fast food." They require very little cooking time and can be purchased in fresh convenient, ready-to-cook forms. Or, if you prefer, you can learn to clean whole fish and shuck shellfish like an expert with just a little practice. Seafood preparation techniques are simple and require only a few basic tools. Fish and shellfish can be cooked by the same methods used for any other type of food, with excellent results.

FISH AND SHELLFISH MARKETING CHECKLIST

FRESH FISH
- Flesh is firm and elastic and doesn't appear separate from the bones.
- Fillets and steaks have a freshly cut appearance and color.
- Odor is fresh and mild, not offensive.
- Eyes are bright, full and often protruding from the head.
- Gills are pinkish red and free of slime.
- Skin is shiny, color has not faded, and scales are firmly attached.
- Flesh springs back when pressed gently.

FROZEN FISH
- Flesh is solidly frozen, with no discoloration.
- There is no odor or an inoffensive, mild odor.
- Wrapping is moisture and vapor resistant, with little or no air space between the fish and the wrapper.
- Package is damage-free and clearly labeled.

FRESH SHRIMP
- Head is closely attached to tail section.
- Shell and flesh are free of black spots.
- Flesh is firm.
- Odor is mild, fresh and clean.

COOKED SHRIMP
- Shell and flesh have a reddish tinge.

FROZEN SHRIMP
- Shrimp is solidly frozen, with no signs of discoloration or freezer burn.
- Shrimp have little or no odor and no black spots.

OYSTERS IN THE SHELL
- Oysters are alive (shells should be closed or close tightly when tapped). A gaping shell indicates that the oyster is dead, and not edible.

SHUCKED OYSTERS
- Flesh is plump and creamy, and the liquid is clear.

CRABS
- Live crabs are moving, are a bright color, and have no disagreeable odor.
- Freshly cleaned crabs are on ice and have no disagreeable odor.
- Frozen soft-shell crabs should be solidly frozen in moisture and vapor resistant wrapping.

SCALLOPS
- Packages contain no excess liquid.
- Odor is sweet.
- Flesh is creamy white, light tan, or pinkish.

LOBSTERS

• Legs should be moving or show movement when touched.
• Tails should curl under the body when picked up.
• Have a fresh, not offensive odor.
• Frozen lobsters and lobster tails should be frozen solid and have no odor.

FISH MARKET FORMS

Whole or round fish are sold just as they come from the water. They must be dressed before cooking.

Chunks are cross sections of large dressed fish, having a cross section of backbone as the only bone.

Drawn fish have had entrails removed. Since entrails cause rapid spoilage, drawn fish have longer storage life.

Steaks are slices of dressed fish smaller than chunks. Salmon, halibut, swordfish and other large fish are commonly sold as steaks.

Dressed fish have head, tails, fins, and viscera removed. With some species, head and tail are left on.

Fillets are sides of the fish cut away from the backbone. Fillets are a good buy because there is no waste.

STORING SEAFOOD

Proper storage is essential to maintain the flavor and nutritive value of fish and shellfish. Purchased fresh fish should be stored in its original wrapping only if you're certain that the wrapping is airtight and moisture resistant. It's safest to re-wrap it yourself in clinging plastic wrap or aluminum foil before placing it in the coldest part of your refrigerator. A damp cloth placed inside the wrapping will prevent it from drying out. If you don't cook the fish within two or three days, it should be frozen.

FREEZING

Whole fish should be cleaned and cut into its final use form (fillets, steaks, chunks, etc.) before it's frozen to save thawing time and utilize your freezer space more efficiently. Carefully package the fish (or fish segments) in clinging plastic wrap, aluminum foil or freezer paper to protect it from oxidation and freezer burn. Make sure you eliminate any air pockets surrounding the fish. If you prefer, you can place the fish uncovered on a tray in the freezer and, when it is frozen solid, dip it in ice water and return it to the freezer. This dipping, repeated several times, results in a fish surrounded by an iced glaze, which protects its flesh while in the freezer.

THAWING

Proper thawing is as important as proper freezing. It's best to thaw a frozen fish in your refrigerator over a pan to catch the water as it drips. Fish should never be thawed at room temperature or under hot water. Thawing a wrapped fish under cold running water can be effective and will not promote bacteria growth in the fish, but it will make the flesh mushy.

SHELLFISH TIPS

CRAB

Crab may be sold live in the shell or dead and cleaned, still in the shell. Blue crab may also be steamed, the meat removed from the shell and sold as fresh crab meat. This crab meat is sold as "lump meat," "flake meat," and "claw meat." The flesh may also be pastuerized, frozen or canned.

HOW TO CLEAN A CRAB

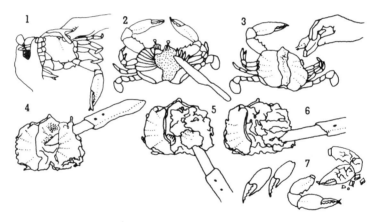

1. With crab upside down, grasp the legs on one side firmly with one hand, and with the other hand lift the flap (apron) and pull back and down to remove the top shell.

2. Turn the crab right side up, remove the gills and wash out the intestines and spongy material.

3. With a twisting motion pull the legs loose from the body. Remove any meat which adheres to the legs. Break off claws.

4. Slice off the top of the inner skeleton and remove all exposed meat on this slice.

5. At the back of the crab, on each side, lies a large lump of meat. With a very careful U-shaped motion of the knife, remove this back fin lump.

6. Remove the white flake meat from the other pockets with the point of the knife.

7. Crack the claw shell and remove the shell along with the moveable pincer. This will expose the claw meat and, if meat is left attached to the remaining pincer, will make a delicious (crab finger) hors d'oeuvre. Or the dark meat can be removed and used in soups, casseroles or salads.

SHRIMP

Fresh caught shrimp will keep for two or three days in crushed ice in the refrigerator. Purchased fresh shrimp will keep for one or two days. If you plan to store shrimp for more than two days, they should be frozen. Before freezing, the heads should be removed and they should be frozen in a block of ice or glazed. When purchasing shrimp, remember that they're sold according to the number of headless shrimp contained in a pound, indicated by the terms jumbo, large, medium and small. Jumbo shrimp have fewer than 15 in a pound, while small indicates 60 or more. Two pounds of raw, headless, unpeeled shrimp will yield one pound of cooked, peeled and de-veined shrimp. If you buy shrimp with heads on, remember that the head makes up approximately 40 percent of the body weight. Raw shrimp may be brown, pink, or white, but after boiling 2-3 minutes the flesh is always white with reddish tinges. You can gauge cooking time by remembering that shrimp flesh is opaque when cooked.

HOW TO SHELL, DE-VEIN AND BUTTERFLY LARGE SHRIMP

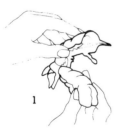
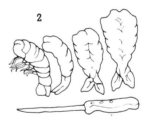

1. Taking a large or jumbo shrimp, cut along its back, making about a ¼″ incision from head to tail. Wash under cold water to remove sand track. Remove shell and legs.

2. Cut the remaining shrimp tail along the back so that it can be split apart and spread open. Be careful not to cut all the way through the tail.

SCALLOPS

Since scallops cannot close their shells tightly as clams and oysters can, they die soon after being removed from the water. Consequently, scallops are always shucked immediately after being harvested, and the meat is sold fresh or frozen. Scallops can be cooked in a variety of ways, but they should always be cooked immediately before serving. If they're allowed to cool, they lose most of their flavor.

HOW TO SHUCK A SCALLOP

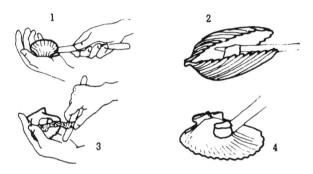

To shuck a scallop, hold it in the palm of one hand with the shell's hinge against the palm.

1. Insert a slender, strong knife, not sharp (a dinner knife will do) between the halves of the shell near the hinge, then twist to give access to the inside. Do not force the shell open as this will tear the scallop muscle.

2. Lift the top side of the shell far enough to insert the knife point and sever the muscle from the top shell. Remove the top shell. Leave the muscle attached to the bottom shell until all viscera is removed.

3. To remove the viscera, grip the dark portion of the scallop firmly between the thumb and knife blade and pull gently. This should remove everything but the edible white scallop muscle.

4. When all viscera is removed, sever the muscle from the remaining shell. Wash the scallop meat in cold water, place in moisture-vapor proof wrapping and ice immediately.

OYSTERS

Although most often served raw on the half shell, oysters can also be baked in the half shell. Remove the top shell and arrange the bottom shell on a bed of rock salt in a round baking tin. Bake at 350°F. 10 minutes.

HOW TO SHUCK AN OYSTER

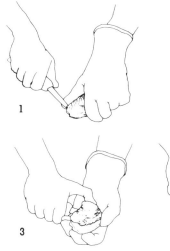

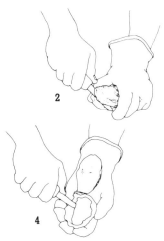

1. Make sure that the shell of the oyster is tightly closed, or that it closes quickly when handled. After scrubbing the shell with a stiff brush, grip the oyster as shown, forcing the shucking knife into the side opposite the hinge.

2. With a twist of the knife blade, slowly force the oyster shell open.

3. With a quick side-to-side motion, slice through the large adductor muscle attached to the flat upper shell (note thumb position).

4. Remove top shell, and cut the lower end of the muscle attached to the bottom half of the shell. Remove shell chips that cling to the meat. The most common way to serve oysters is on the half shell with lemon. If not served immediately, place oysters in a container, cover them with their own liquid, and refrigerate.

CLAMS

Clams are most often purchased live in the shell, and are ideal for steaming. First, rinse the clams well in cold running water to remove sand and dirt. The clean clams should be placed in a large pot. Place one or two inches of water (or other liquid) in the pot, cover tightly, and steam until the clams on top open slightly.

HOW TO SHUCK A CLAM

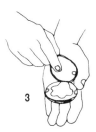

1. Like an oyster shell, a clam shell should be tightly closed, indicating that the clam is alive and edible. Hold the clam as shown and insert knife betwen halves of the shell.

2. Cut around the clam, using a twisting motion to loosen the shell and pry it open.

3. Serve on the half shell, taking care not to lose any of the delicious juice. Clams on the half shell must be served very cold.

LOBSTERS

To boil live lobsters, place them in a large pot containing about three inches of briskly boiling salted water. Cover the pot immediately after adding lobsters. After the water boils again, cook for 18 to 20 minutes. They can be served hot or cold.

Before broiling or baking a lobster, cross its large claws, one over the other, and hold them firmly in one hand. Make a deep incision with a sharp, pointed knife at a point between the claws. Draw the knife quickly through the entire length of the body and tail. Remove intestinal vein and craw. There are a variety of stuffings that can be placed in the lobster's body cavity before cooking. Lobster should be broiled for 25-30 minutes, or baked at 350°F. to 400°F. for 30-40 minutes.

HOW TO EAT A LOBSTER

1. Twist off claws where they join the body. Then break off small pincer and discard. Use your fingers.

2. Break claw in two at dotted line, and crack with nutcracker. Lots of people consider this the choice meat. Dip it in drawn butter. Or squeeze on lemon. You'll never forget your first taste.

3. Dig out meat with small fork. Or use your fingers. Or get some help from the nutcracker. Get every little bit.

4. Twist off tail at dotted line, then twist off flippers and discard. Don't worry if you can't do it perfectly the first time.

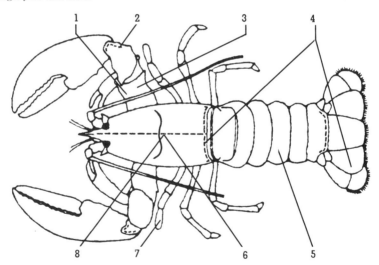

5. Remove meat from tail. Hold the big end and push your small fork in about 1/3 of the way down. Then pull. The meat should come out in one big hunk. On the other hand, some people get it out by simply pushing it through from the small end to the big end. Whatever works is fine.

6. Unhinge the back shell from the body. The liver is in the back and is considered a great delicacy by lobster aficionados. But not everyone likes it. It is all right to leave it.

7. Remove small claws. And bite off each end. There's meat inside that may be sucked out as if using a straw. It is not ill-mannered to do so.

8. Crack the remaining part of the body along dotted line. And remove meat with small fork. If you prefer to leave the body alone, that's OK, too.

CLEANING AND DRESSING FRESH FISH

Immediately upon getting your fish home, clean and dress it. Remember to handle it gently; fish flesh is delicate.

The amount of cleaning depends on variety of fish and use intended. There are dozens of gadgets for cleaning fish. Usually a sharp knife and some practice will do the job.

Fish, just as they come from the water, are whole or round fish.

SCALES

Fish vary in number of scales and difficulty of removal. Trout have few scales to remove. Carp have scales which make a coat of armor and have to be "sawed" off or removed with the skin.

Generally fish are scaled by this method. Lay fish on the table. With one hand, hold the fish firmly by the head. Holding the knife almost vertical, scrape off the scales working from tail to head. A quick dip in boiling water will make scaling easier and also helps remove the slime layer.

SKIN

The skin is removed from bullheads, catfish, burbot, and other fish. Hold the head firmly or nail it to a board. Slit the skin down the back and around the fins. Use pliers to pull off the skin. Pull from head to tail.

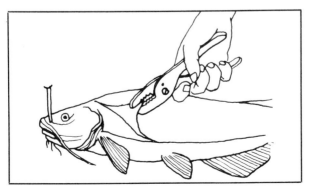

GUTTING

Fish with gills and viscera removed are *drawn* fish. Cut the entire length of the fish belly from vent to head and remove the viscera. Be sure to remove all dark material next to the backbone; this is the kidney. A stiff-bristled brush will help remove remains difficult to get with a knife. Then rinse thoroughly with clean water. (Save the fish liver. Though often no larger than the end of your thumb, fish livers can be tasty. Sauté them in butter or add them to scrambled eggs.)

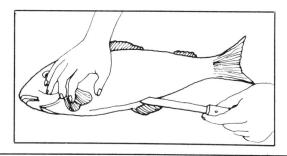

HEAD

Fish is often cooked with the head on, especially with large fish. Then the gills must be removed. Insert tip of knife into gill cover and pull out gills and gill rackers.

To remove the head, cut just above the collarbone behind the pectoral fins. If the backbone is large, cut down to it and then snap it over the edge of a table or cutting board. Cut any remaining flesh holding the head to the body. Remove the cheek meat from large fish.

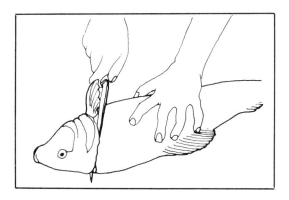

CLEANING THE HEAD

The head can be useful for making stock and soups. Remove the gills and gill rackers and wash thoroughly. It is not necessary to remove the eyes. Don't forget the cheek meat. It is delicious.

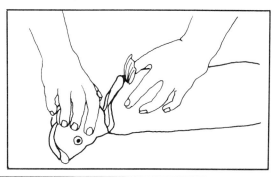

FINS

Remove the dorsal (large back) fin by cutting along both sides of the fin. Then give a quick pull toward the head and pull out the fin with the root bones attached. Remove other fins in the same way.

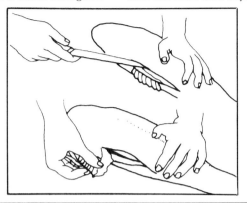

WASHING

The fish is now pan-dressed. Wash thoroughly in cold drinking-quality water. Store on ice or in the refrigerator.

COOKING FORMS

STEAKS.

Fish can be cut into other forms. Large fish are often steaked. Cut crosswise, parallel to ribs. Make steaks about 1 inch thick.

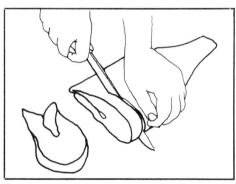

Cutting steaks

FILLETS.

If you plan to fillet, it isn't necessary to gut the fish. Just fillet as described here, and remove fins and split into two pieces. To make butterfly fillets, you won't even split the fillets or cut through the belly.

Filleting requires a sharp, thin-bladed knife. Cut through the flesh along the back from tail to just behind the head. Then cut down to the backbone just above the collarbone. Turn the knife flat and cut the flesh along the backbone to the tail, allowing the knife to run over the rib bones. Lift off the entire side of the fish in one piece. Turn the fish over and repeat the operation on the other side. To skin a fillet, lay it on the cutting board skin-side down. Hold the tail end with your fingers and cut through the flesh to the skin. Flatten the knife on the skin and cut the flesh away, running the knife forward while holding the free end of skin firmly in your fingers.

Save bones, heads and skin to use in fish stock.

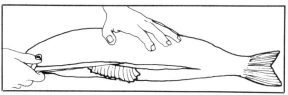

1. Start filleting by cutting along back.

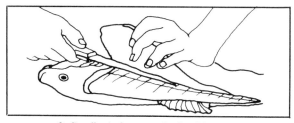

2. Cut flesh down to the backbone.

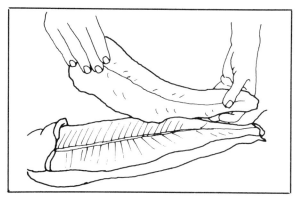

3. Lift off the side in one piece.

BONES.

There are a number of ways to reduce bone problems. Canning fish softens bones so they are edible. Or you can grind them up in minced flesh. Fillet the bony fish like mullet. Put fillets through a meat grinder fitted with a fine blade. Use minced flesh in fish loaves, soups, casseroles and other dishes.

You can fry the bones crisp. Fillet the fish. Lay fillets on cutting board, skin-side down. Every ⅛ to ¼ inch, cut crosswise through the fillet, but do not cut through the skin. Bread or batter the fillet and fry in a generous amount of oil.

You can remove the bones from cooked fillets. Cut along the solid lines in the drawing to remove the strips of Y bones.

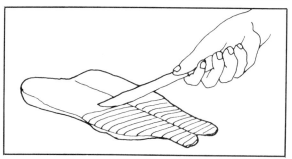

Cross-cut fillets to reduce size
of small bones.

BASIC FISH COOKERY

Cook fish promptly—Never keep raw fish longer than three days in the refrigerator.

Cooking frozen fish—You can cook fish quite successfully without thawing it first. Just allow additional cooking time for the frozen fish—about double the time in the recipe. But, recipes which call for stuffing, breading or broiling work better if the fish is thawed first. Thaw fish in its original wrappings in the refrigerator. Allow 16 to 18 hours per pound. Thaw fish only until it has just become pliable. It may still have some ice crystals in it. Never refreeze fish.

Cook to develop flavor—Fish flesh is very delicate and should be cooked only long enough to develop flavor. As a general rule, use low to moderate heat. Fish should be heated to an internal temperature of at least 180°F.

Overcooking is the most common mistake—Fish is done when white or cream-colored compared with the semi-transparent look of raw fish. It flakes easily when tested with a fork. If it falls apart by itself, it is overcooked. Properly cooked, it has a fine flavor and is moist, tender, and flaky. Overcooking makes fish tough, dry, and rubbery.

SERVING GUIDES

Allow 3 to 4 ounces of cooked fish per serving. The chart shows how much fish of each form you would need. It is only a guide. You will need to vary serving size to suit the size of appetites in your family.

FORM	1 SERVING	4 SERVINGS
Dressed or pan-dressed	½ lb.	2 lbs.
Fillets or steaks	⅓ lb.	1-⅓ lbs.
Portions	2 portions	8 portions
Sticks	4 sticks	16 sticks
Canned	⅙ lb.	⅔ lb.

SUBSTITUTING FISH IN RECIPES

Most recipes work equally well with any kind of fish. Two things to remember, however, when substituting one fish for another are size and fat content.

Size—Smaller fish cook faster than larger fish. For example, when substituting several smaller fillets for one large fillet, test for doneness early and often. Size is also related to fat content. Small fish of a species tend to have less fat than a larger fish of the same kind.

Fat content—Most white-fleshed fish have lean, mild meat. Dark-fleshed fish tend to be oilier and more strongly flavored. If you substitute fat for fat and lean for lean, you will not need to alter recipes. Lean fish may require more oil in the recipe or extra basting than a fatter fish cooked by the same method. Strongly flavored fish may require extra seasoning. A cooking method which reduces oil reduces strong flavors.

Lean fish include: alewife, bass, brook trout, bullheads, bluegills, burbot, carp, catfish, crappies, lake herring, northern pike, sucker, sunfish, walleye, and yellow perch. Lean fish often seen in cookbook recipes are: cod, haddock, ocean perch, sole, turbot, and red snapper. Fat fish include: chubs, lake trout, rainbow trout, chinook salmon, and coho salmon.

FISH COOKERY METHODS

BROILING

Broiling renders oils out of the fish, so it is best used with fatty fish. Dressed fish, steaks, or fillets about 1 inch thick are suggested. Lean fish may require extra basting, or you can water broil them instead.

BROILING

METHOD
1. Grease a shallow baking pan or broiler rack or cover with aluminum foil.
2. Preheat broiler.
3. Place fish on broiler pan and brush with melted butter, margarine or oil.
4. Salt and pepper the fish.
5. Place pan under the broiler so that the surface of fish is 3 to 4 inches from heat.
6. Cook until fish flakes with fork in thickest portion, usually about 10 minutes.
7. Serve sizzling hot.

Follow same procedure for pan-dressed fish except turn them once about half way through the cooking at 5 to 8 minutes.

BAKING

Baking is one of the easiest ways to cook fish, though not always the quickest.

BAKING

METHOD

1. Rub fish inside and out with salt.
2. Place fish in a greased baking pan.
3. Brush with melted fat, or lay slices of bacon over top.
4. Bake in a moderate oven (350° F.) for 45 to 60 minutes or until fish flakes easily.
5. If fish seems dry during baking, brush occasionally with drippings or melted fat, or baste with sauce.
6. Serve immediately on a hot platter, plain or with a sauce.

Dressed baked fish is excellent stuffed. Use rice, bread, or herb stuffing. Fillets or steaks may be baked by the same procedure. Reduce the time to 20 to 25 minutes.

See "Cooking Fish in Liquid" for baking fish in sauces.

NO-STICK TRICKS

To prevent fish sticking to pan, make a bed of celery tops or other vegetables. Lay fish on the vegetable bed. Coat cold pan with fat. Sprinkle it with corn meal. Lay fish in pan and cook.

Fish is usually more moist if head and tail of whole fish are left on for baking.

PLANKING

This is how a fish is often served in restaurants. No extra serving dishes are needed. Simply cook the fish on the serving dish.

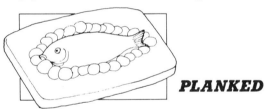

PLANKED

METHOD

1. Clean, wash and dry fish.
2. Sprinkle fish inside with salt and pepper.
3. Place on a preheated, oiled plank or well-greased bake-and-serve platter.
4. Brush fish with melted fat or oil.
5. Bake in a moderate oven (350°F.) for 45 to 60 minutes or until fish flakes easily when tested with a fork.
6. Serve with mashed potatoes and vegetables arranged on plank or platter.

Pan-dressed fish will require only 25 to 30 minutes.

Fillets and steaks can also be planked. Reduce cooking time to 20 to 25 minutes.

FRYING

Frying methods all use oil for a crispy surface for the fish. It is very important to have hot, but not smoking, oil. Heating the oil until it smokes will give the fish off-flavors. Fish should be fried in hot fat at 350° to 375°F.

PAN FRY

PAN FRYING

1. Cut fish into servings if too large to fry whole.
2. Coat with flour and seasonings or other coating mixture. (See "Batter and Breadings.")
3. Place fish in a heavy frying pan with about ⅛ inch melted fat, hot but not smoking.
4. Keep fat hot but not smoking.
5. When fish is brown on one side, turn carefully and brown the other.
6. Cooking takes about 5 minutes on each side, depending on the thickness of the fish.
7. Drain on absorbent paper.
8. Serve immediately on a hot platter, plain or with sauce.

OVEN FRY

OVEN FRYING (PORTIONS)

1. Preheat oven to 500°F.
2. Cut fish into serving-size portions.
3. Dip in salted milk, and coat in crumbs.
4. Grease a shallow baking pan.
5. Place fish in pan, and pour a little melted butter, margarine or oil over fish.
6. Cook 10 to 15 minutes or until fish flake easily.

Oven frying requires little time and no careful watching. The high temperatures and crumb coating keep fish moist and give it an attractive brown crust.

DEEP FAT FRY

1. Cut fish into servings.
2. Dip in batter or coating mixture.
3. Fill a deep kettle with enough fat to cover the fish, but no more than half full.
4. Heat the fat to 350°F.
5. Place a layer of fish in the frying basket.
6. Cook to an even golden brown, about 3 to 5 minutes.
7. Raise basket, remove fish and drain on absorbent paper.
8. Serve immediately, plain or with sauce.

STEAMING

This is a good way to prepare fish for persons on restricted diets, and to cook fish for cooked fish dishes.

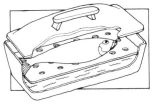

STEAMING

STOVE TOP STEAMING

1. Sprinkle fish with salt and pepper.
2. Bring liquid to boil in a deep pan.
3. Place fish on rack over boiling water.
4. Cover pan.
5. Steam 5 to 10 minutes.

OVEN STEAMING

1. Wipe fish with damp cloth and season with salt and pepper.
2. Measure thickness of fish.
3. Wrap fish tightly in an envelope of greased aluminum foil. Double fold and pinch ends to make foil steam tight.
4. Place on baking sheet in moderate oven (350°F).
5. Allow 10 minutes per inch of thickness for fresh fish and 20 minutes per inch for frozen fish.

WATER BROILING

This method is ideal for lean fish. It combines the moistness of steaming with the desirable appearance of broiling.

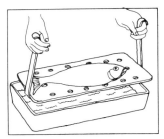

WATER BROILING

METHOD

1. Preheat broiler pan with oven.
2. Bring water or other steaming liquid to a boil.
3. Remove rack from pan. Pour liquid into lower portion of pan, to at least ¼ inch deep. Make sure some space remains between liquid and broiler rack.
4. Grease rack lightly.
5. Place fish on rack. If desired, cover with topping or dot with butter.
6. Return pan to oven, about 3 to 4 inches from heat. Broil fish about 8 minutes. Check early to see if it's done. If top browns before fish flakes easily, turn off broiler and let the steam finish the cooking.

Thin fillets or steaks (about ¾ inch) work better than thick pieces. Use water, lemon juice and water, wine, court bouillon or any other liquid that produces adequate steam.

COOKING FISH IN LIQUID

Liquid cooking is especially good for lean fish. Retain cooking liquids for sauces and soups.

POACHING
1. Place fish in saucepan. Put fish in a basket or cheesecloth for easy handling.
2. Barely cover with liquid.
3. Simmer—do not boil—5 to 10 minutes or until fish flakes easily.
4. Remove and serve, or flake for use in other dishes.

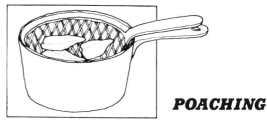

POACHING

Burbot is good cut into strips and poached and then eaten like lobster dipped in melted butter.

IN SAUCES — STOVE-TOP
1. Place fish in frying pan.
2. Cover with sauce.
3. Simmer 10 minutes or until fish flakes easily.

IN SAUCES — OVEN
1. Place fillet in baking dish in single layer.
2. Cover with sauce.
3. Place in moderate oven (350° F).
4. Cook about 20 minutes or until fish flakes with fork. Double the time for frozen fish.

OUTDOOR FLAVOR

Fish tastes especially good when grilled. Add an outdoor flavor at home by cooking fish on a charcoal grill, but never use a grill indoors. Always cook fish over burned-down coals. Fish cook quickly and are naturally tender, so they are well suited to outdoor cookery. (And outdoor cooking also means no kitchen odors.)

FILLETS OR STEAKS
1. Place fish on one half of wire grill.
2. Baste with butter or sauce.
3. Close grill and place about 4 inches above coals.
4. Broil 10 to 20 minutes, turning fish once.

Fish sticks to the grill and is apt to fall apart when you try to turn it. To avoid this problem, use a long-handled, mesh basket or hinged grill, or encase the fish in aluminum foil, or spread foil over the regular grill and lay fish on the foil. To let oils drain away, pierce the foil in several places.

Thick cuts dry out less readily than thin cuts.

DRESSED FISH

1. Wrap a 2 lb. to 3 lb. dressed fish in aluminum foil.
2. Place it on the grill.
3. Cook slowly 30 to 40 minutes, turning fish occasionally.

FISH COOKING GUIDE

COOKING METHOD	FORM	AMOUNT FOR FOUR	TEMPERATURE (F)	TIME IN MINUTES
BAKING & PLANKING	dressed	2 lb.	350°F.	45 to 60
	pan-dressed	2 lb.	350°F.	25 to 30
	fillets or steaks	1⅓ lb.	350°F.	20 to 25
	frozen breaded portions	8 portions	400°F.	15 to 20
	frozen fried sticks	16 sticks	400°F.	15 to 20
BROILING	dressed	2 lb.		10 to 16 (turn once)
	pan-dressed	2 lb.	broil 3 to 4 inches	10 to 16 (turn once)
	fillets or steaks	1⅓ lb.	from heat	10 to 15
	portions and sticks	8 and 16		10 to 15
WATER BROILING	thin fillets or steaks	1⅓ lb.	same as broil	6 to 10
CHARCOAL BROILING	dressed (foil-wrapped)	2 lb.	burned-down coals 3 to 4 inches	30 to 40 (turn)
	pan-dressed	2 lb.	from heat	30 to 40 (turn)
	fillets or steaks	1⅓ lb.		10 to 20 (turn once)
POACHING	fillets or steaks	1⅓ lb.	simmer	5 to 10
STEAMING	fillets or steaks	1⅓ lb.	boil	5 to 10
OVEN FRYING	pan-dressed	2 lb.	500°F.	15 to 20
	fillets or steaks	1⅓ lb.	500°F.	10 to 15
PAN FRYING	pan-dressed	2 lb.		
	fillets or steaks	1⅓ lb.	moderate	8 to 10 (turn once)
	breaded, fried portions	8		
	breaded, fried sticks	16		
DEEP FAT FRYING	pan-dressed	2 lb.		
	fillets or steaks	1⅓ lb.	350°F.	3 to 5
	raw breaded portions	8		

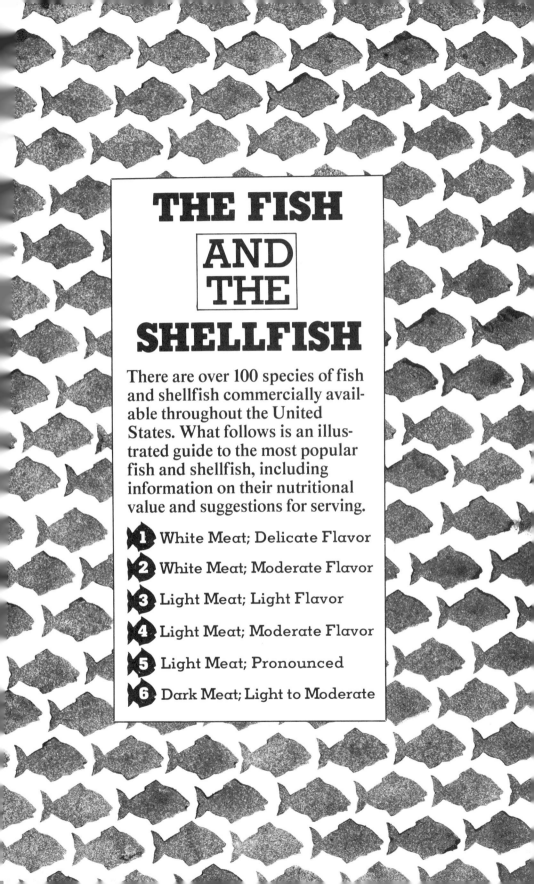

THE FISH

AND THE

SHELLFISH

There are over 100 species of fish and shellfish commercially available throughout the United States. What follows is an illustrated guide to the most popular fish and shellfish, including information on their nutritional value and suggestions for serving.

1 White Meat; Delicate Flavor

2 White Meat; Moderate Flavor

3 Light Meat; Light Flavor

4 Light Meat; Moderate Flavor

5 Light Meat; Pronounced

6 Dark Meat; Light to Moderate

More than 100 of the best-known and most commercially important fish and shellfish are described in the pages that follow. The fish are categorized according to edibility profiles—all fish in the same section share similar taste qualities. This enables you to compare the flavor of fish you've never tasted with the flavor of fish you're familiar with. The categories are:

1. *White meat fish with light, delicate flavor;*
2. *White meat fish with moderate, somewhat stronger flavor;*
3. *Light meat fish (the flesh is slightly darker than that of the white meat fish) with light flavor;*
4. *Light meat fish with moderate, somewhat stronger flavor;*
5. *Light meat fish with strong, pronounced flavor;*
6. *Dark meat fish with flavor that ranges from light to moderate.*

Within each of the edibility categories, fish are divided alphabetically according to the family to which they belong. If a specific fish is a member of a large and/or especially well-known subfamily, it has been classified by the subgroup rather than the broader family. For example, although salmon and trout both belong to the larger trout family, they are listed separately under "salmon" and "trout"; sea trout are members of the drum family, but they are listed under the subgroup "sea trout." If you're looking for a specific fish and aren't sure of its family, check the chapter index. Shellfish are divided only according to family, not according to edibility characteristics.

For each of the fish and shellfish, you'll find a Latin name, common names and, in the case of fin fish and lobsters, average weight. For each species, there is a general information about the fish, including a physical description, its commercial importance, historical or cultural significance and other pertinent information.

Below the general information, you'll find a description of where the fish lives, including its general range and, where available, the depth, environment and water temperatures that it prefers.

Each profile lists the species' peak harvesting season—not necessarily the only time it is available fresh, but the months in which it is most likely to be abundant and readily accessible.

There is information on the most effective methods and baits commonly used to catch each fish and shellfish. In the case of commercially important species, the methods used by professional fishing vessels are included as well.

Under the "Availability" heading is a list of the forms in which the fish can usually be purchased in retail stores. "Nutritive Value" offers information on the protein levels and nutrients of each species, and "Best Ways to Serve It" suggests the cooking methods to which each species is best suited.

INDEX

49

ATLANTIC CODFISH

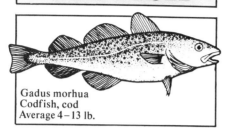

Gadus morhua
Codfish, cod
Average 4 – 13 lb.

About The Atlantic Codfish: Shortly after Columbus' voyage to the "New World," fishermen in sailing ships began crossing the Atlantic in search of a reported abundance of fish. The most abundant was probably cod, and exploitation of the cod resource began in the 16th century when French and Portuguese ships fished off Newfound-land. Cod comprised a large part of the American colonists' diet. A model of a codfish, cast in gold, hangs in the Massachusetts statehouse.

Where It's Caught: The codfish is found in the Atlantic Ocean from Virginia to the Arctic. It is most plentiful in the Gulf of St. Lawrence, off Newfoundland, and is usually found near the ocean floor, especially around slopes and shoals.

When It's Caught: Cod can be caught year round in depths of more than 180 feet. Recreational fishermen usually catch it between June and November in depths of 60 to 300 feet.

How It's Caught: Bottom fishing from boats. Baits include squid, crabs, clams, worms and cut fish.

Availability: Whole, steaks, fillets, sticks; fresh and frozen.

Nutritive Value: High in protein, low in fat.

Best Ways To Serve It: Broiled or baked.

HADDOCK

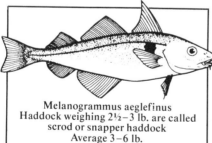

Melanogrammus aeglefinus
Haddock weighing 2½ – 3 lb. are called scrod or snapper haddock
Average 3 – 6 lb.

About The Haddock: A member of the cod family, the haddock is an important commercial fish. It is particularly well-known as "finnan haddie," the famous smoked haddock of Scotland. The haddock looks very much like a codfish but is considerably smaller.

Where It's Caught: Haddock is found on both sides of the Atlantic, as far west as New England and as far east as the northern part of the Bay of Biscay. North to south, it ranges from Iceland to Cape Hatteras, North Carolina. It is found in water temperatures of 34°F. to 60°F. and in depths up to 600 feet. It especially likes to inhabit ledges and rocky outcroppings near the bottom.

When It's Caught: Year round in depths of more than 240 feet; from April through October in shallower waters.

How It's Caught: Bottom fishing from anchored or slow-drifting boats. Baits include squid, clams, mussels, worms and cut fish.

Availability: Whole, dressed, fillets, portions; fresh and frozen; smoked.

Nutritive Value: High in protein.

Best Ways To Serve It: Baked or broiled. Smoked haddock lends itself to poaching.

About The Scrod: Often found on restaurant menus and in cookbooks, "scrod" is not a species of fish but the commercial name used to market codfish that weigh less than three pounds. Another member of the cod family, the haddock, may also be known as scrod when it weighs less than three pounds. These smaller fish tend to have a more delicate flavor than the larger cod or haddock.

Where It's Caught: The Atlantic Ocean, from Virginia to the Arctic. It is most plentiful in the Gulf of St. Lawrence, off Newfoundland. Scrod and larger codfish and haddock are usually found near the bottom, especially around slopes and shoals.

When It's Caught: Year round in depths of more than 180 feet. Recreational fishermen usually catch them between June and November in

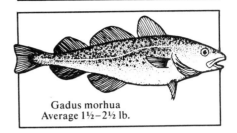

SCROD

Gadus morhua
Average 1½–2½ lb.

depths of 60 to 300 feet.

How It's Caught: Bottom fishing from boats. Baits include squid, crabs, clams, worms and cut fish.

Availability: Whole, fillets; fresh and frozen.

Nutritive Value: High in protein, low in fat.

Best Ways To Serve It: Broiled or baked.

FLOUNDER

About The The Southern Flounder: A close relative of the summer flounder (fluke), the southern flounder is olive in color with a white underside. It is a left-eye flounder.

Where It's Caught: The southern flounder is found from North Carolina to Texas in shallow water near mud bottoms. In the Gulf of Mexico it is found in environments ranging from mild salt water to full-strength seawater. The greatest concentrations of southern flounder occurs in bays where fresh water is mixed with salt water.

When It's Caught: Year round in shallow coastal waters.

How It's Caught: Many are caught by shrimp trawlers during the spring. Sport fishermen use a flashlight or torch to lure the southern flounder close to shore, then spear it as it swims in shallow water.

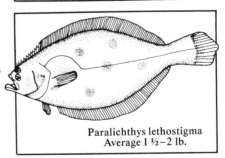

SOUTHERN FLOUNDER

Paralichthys lethostigma
Average 1 ½–2 lb.

Availability: Whole, dressed, fillets, breaded; fresh or frozen.

Nutritive Value: High in protein, thiamine and niacin.

Best Ways To Serve It: Fried, sautéed or broiled.

WINDOWPANE FLOUNDER

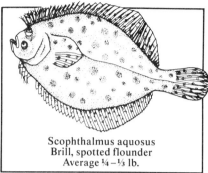

Scophthalmus aquosus
Brill, spotted flounder
Average ¼–⅓ lb.

About The Windowpane
Flounder: The windowpane flounder is so named because its body is so thin it allows light to shine through it. It is considered more a game fish than a commercial fish because of its extremely light weight and high ratio of bones to meat, which make it somewhat impractical for cooking. A few occasionally find their way to market. The windowpane flounder is red to grayish brown with dark brown spots scattered across its body.

Where It's Caught: Along the Atlantic coast of North America, from the Gulf of St. Lawrence to South Carolina. It is a bottom dweller.

When It's Caught: During the spring and summer months.

How It's Caught: Lines from shore or boats. Baits include cut fish and artificial lures.

Availability: Little or no commercial availability. The windowpane flounder is eaten primarily by sport fishermen.

Nutritive Value: High in protein, thiamine and niacin.

Best Ways To Serve It: Fried or sautéed.

YELLOWTAIL FLOUNDER

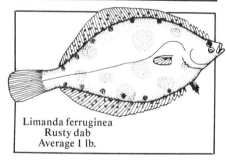

Limanda ferruginea
Rusty dab
Average 1 lb.

About The Yellowtail
Flounder: This right-eye flounder is easily recognized by its small mouth and pointed snout. It can be grayish green or reddish in color, with large rust-color spots running along its body. Its underside is white with yellow markings.

Where It's Caught: Along the Atlantic coast from Labrador to Virginia, although it is more abundant in the north Atlantic than the south. It can be found in depths of 30 to 300 feet, and seems to prefer a sandy or sand-and-mud bottom.

When It's Caught: March through August.

How It's Caught: The yellowtail flounder is an extremely important part of the fishing industry, and commercial vessels usually catch it in otter trawls. Recreational fishermen occasionally catch yellowtails with lines from drifting boats, using squid and worms as bait.

Availability: Whole, dressed, fillets; fresh and frozen.

Nutritive Value: High in protein, thiamine and niacin.

Best Ways to Serve It: Fried, sautéed or broiled.

About The Fluke: The fluke is a member of a large family of flatfish that includes winter flounder, summer flounder, starry flounder, yellowtail flounder and a variety of sole and dab. Flounder are highly prized by sport as well as commercial fishermen.

Where It's Found: Fluke inhabit almost every coastline of the United States. Most members of the flounder family live along the continental shelf and slope, although some venture into shallower waters and are found in bays near shore along the coast. They usually feed near the bottom, but occasionally surface in search of food.

When It's Caught: Late April through December in water 61°F. or warmer. Fishing is best from July through September.

How It's Caught: Bottom fishing from shore, bottom trolling from

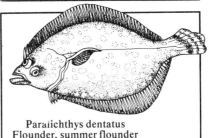

FLUKE

Paralichthys dentatus
Flounder, summer flounder
Average 1–3 lb. (more than 11 lb. is unusual)

boats; chumming. Baits include killifish, squid, clams, worms and cut fish.

Availability: Fillets (most flounder and sole); fresh and frozen.

Nutritive Value: High in protein, low in fat.

Best Ways To Serve It: Pan-fried, broiled or sautéed.

About The Atlantic Halibut: This extremely large member of the right-eye flounder family can reach weights of up to 700 pounds, although halibut over 300 pounds is considered unusual. Female Atlantic halibut tend to be larger than males. The fish can range from olive to grayish brown to deep brown, and the underside is usually white, although there may be dark markings on larger fish. Atlantic halibut grow very slowly — a three-year-old fish may be only a foot long, but a 20-year-old halibut may be about five feet long.

Where It's Caught: The Atlantic halibut is found in the cool sections of the Atlantic Ocean — from New Jersey as far south as Virginia, and from Greenland down the northern coast of Europe as far south as the English Channel. It prefers sand, gravel and clay bottoms to mud. It is found in depths ranging from 200 to 3,000 feet, and in water temperatures of 40° to 50°F.

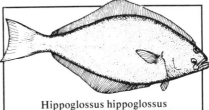

ATLANTIC HALIBUT

Hippoglossus hippoglossus
Fish under 50 lb. are called chicken halibut
Average 30 — 85 lb.

When It's Caught: Year round in depths of more than 300 feet.

How It's Caught: Bottom fishing from boats. Baits include live or cut fish, squid, crabs and clams.

Availability: Fillets, steaks; fresh and frozen.

Nutritive Value: High in protein, niacin and vitamin A.

Best Ways To Serve It: Broiled or baked.

PACIFIC SANDDAB

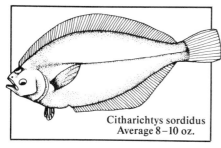

Citharichtys sordidus
Average 8–10 oz.

About The Pacific Sanddab:
A left-eye flounder, the tiny Pacific sanddab is one of the most sought-after of all flatfish because of its excellent eating qualities. The Pacific sanddab is tan or brown in color and may have orange or black patches. Like most flatfish, the sanddab spends most of its time near the bottom, but it can move very quickly in pursuit of small fish and crustaceans for food.

Where It's Caught: Along the Pacific coast from southern California to northwestern Alaska. It's usually found in depths of 120 to 300 feet, but is occasionally caught in depths of 60 to 600 feet.

When It's Caught: Year round.

How It's Caught: Lines from boats and shore; trawls. Baits include cut fish, squid, shrimp and crabs.

Availability: Whole; usually fresh.

Nutritive Value: High in protein.

Best Ways To Serve It: Pan-fried.

DOVER SOLE

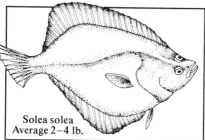

Solea solea
Average 2–4 lb.

About The Dover Sole: The true Dover sole is a European flounder found from the Mediterranean Sea to the north of Scotland and south of Norway. It is found in the mouth of the Baltic Sea, and in the North Sea and the Bay of Biscay. Dover, England, was once the central marketplace of Dover sole for all of England, and eventually lent its name to the fish. The Dover sole is a superb eating fish, and some North American restaurants and retailers purchase imported Dover sole for their customers. If you encounter "Dover sole" on a menu or in a fishmarket, though, ask if it's been imported from Europe. Usually you'll find that the term refers to a Pacific right-eye flounder that's called "dover sole" in North America. While not as extraordinary as the "real" Dover sole, the California version is considered an excellent eating fish and is an important part of the commercial fishing industry.

Where It's Caught: The domestic dover sole can be found in depths between 100 and 3,000 feet in waters off southern California to northwestern Alaska. It is a bottom dweller.

When It's Caught: During the summer months.

How It's Caught: Lines from shore or boats. Baits include shrimp and cut fish.

Availability: Both the European Dover sole and the Pacific dover sole are usually found as fillets; fresh and frozen.

Nutritive Value: Both are high in protein and niacin.

Best Ways To Serve It: Both can be fried, sautéed or broiled.

About The Petrale Sole: A right-eye flounder, the petrale sole is generally considered the most important of all the Pacific flatfish. Like many flatfish, the petrale sole is olive-brown in color with pale patches. Its upper jaw contains two rows of teeth.

Where It's Caught: Along the Pacific coast from the Mexican border to northwest Alaska, in depths from 60 to 1,300 feet.

When It's Caught: During the summer months.

How It's Caught: Lines from boats or shore. Baits include shrimp, squid, cut fish and artificial lures.

Availability: Fillets; fresh and frozen.

Nutritive Value: High in protein and niacin.

Best Ways To Serve It: Fried, sautéed or broiled.

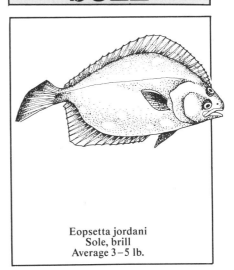

PETRALE SOLE

Eopsetta jordani
Sole, brill
Average 3–5 lb.

About The The Rex Sole: The rex sole's slender body helps to distinguish it from other flatfish, which tend to be rounder. This right-eye flounder is brownish, with a white underside. Although the rex is not as plentiful as other sole and flounder, it has an excellent flavor and comprises a small but vital part of the commercial fishing industry.

Where It's Caught: Along the Pacific coast from California to the Bering Sea. Some are found in relatively shallow water, but most are found in depths of 60 to 800 feet, and some are caught off the coast of Alaska at 2,100 feet.

When It's Caught: During the summer months.

How It's Caught: Lines from boats and shore; trawling. Baits include shrimp, squid and cut fish.

Availability: Unlike most flatfish, the rex sole is too thin to fillet. It is usually sold whole; fresh and frozen.

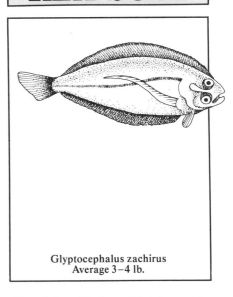

REX SOLE

Glyptocephalus zachirus
Average 3–4 lb.

Nutritive Value: High in protein and niacin.

Best Ways To Serve It: Fried, sautéed or broiled.

SALMON

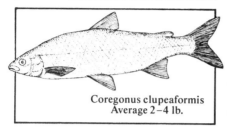

LAKE WHITEFISH

Coregonus clupeaformis
Average 2–4 lb.

About The Lake Whitefish:
The green and silvery lake white-fish is known as "the king of fresh water fish." It is especially important in the state of Michigan, where it is eaten more than any other species. The lake whitefish is a member of the salmon family.

Where It's Caught: In deep lakes from Maine to Minnesota. It prefers to live near rocky outcrop-pings on the lake's bottom.

When It's Caught: May through September.

How It's Caught: Lines from boats; nets.

Availability: Whole, drawn, dressed, fillets; fresh and frozen; smoked.

Nutritive Value: Whitefish flesh is fatty but high in protein and low in cholesterol.

Best Ways To Serve It: Baked or broiled.

SNAPPER

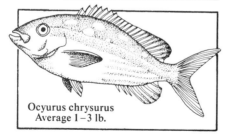

YELLOWTAIL SNAPPER

Ocyurus chrysurus
Average 1–3 lb.

About The Yellowtail Snap-per: A member of the 250 species snapper family, the yellowtail is not-able for its colors. Its body is a pale yellow with a bright yellow stripe running from its head to its back fin, which is also bright yellow. The yellowtail has a reputation as a breakfast fish, gained in Key West in the early 1900's when yellowtails caught during the night were sold by street vendors early in the morning.

Where It's Caught: Most are found in the Gulf of Mexico, but some are found along the Atlantic coast as far north as New York. Their habits are somewhat mysterious, but it appears that they move into shallower coastal waters during the summer months and head back out to sea in the fall. They are believed to spawn in deep water in the late sum-mer and fall.

When It's Caught: May through August.

How It's Caught: Snappers feed at night, so most are caught after sundown. The best bait is cut fish; because the yellowtail has a small mouth, a small hook should be used.

Availability: Whole, fillets; fresh and frozen.

Nutritive Value: High in protein.

Best Ways To Serve It: Boiled, steamed or poached.

BUTTERFISH

About The Butterfish: There are two theories concerning how the butterfish got its name — one claims the name comes from the fish's high fat content; the other says it comes from the protective mucus coating on the fish's skin. The butterfish is a dull black color.

Where It's Caught: Along the Atlantic coast from Nova Scotia to the Gulf of Mexico. On the West coast, pompanos (small blue/green fish) are sometimes sold under the name "butterfish."

When It's Caught: May through October.

How It's Caught: A major commercial fish, the butterfish is usually caught with an otter trawl.

Availability: Fillets, fresh or frozen.

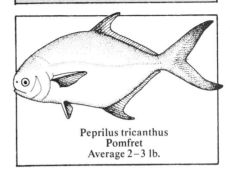

Peprilus tricanthus
Pomfret
Average 2–3 lb.

Nutritive Value: High in fat and protein, low in cholesterol.

Best Ways To Serve It: Fried, sautéed or broiled; especially good in any recipe designed for mackerel.

CATFISH

About The Channel Catfish: Although catfish are accepted as food fish only in the southern and central states, millions are caught and eaten each year — more than in any other country in the world. Catfish are beginning to be featured on menus in major northern cities, including San Francisco, Chicago and New York, and in those areas the demand for catfish exceeds the supply. Of the 28 species of catfish found in North American waters, the freshwater channel catfish is the most commercially important.

Where It's Caught: In the Great Lakes, and in lakes and streams southward to Virginia and west to Mexico. The channel catfish prefers lakes with sandy bottoms and boulders, and avoids heavily weeded areas. It usually feeds at night.

When It's Caught: Year round.

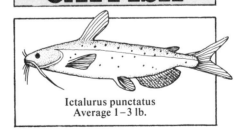

Ictalurus punctatus
Average 1–3 lb.

How It's Caught: Lines from boats and shore. Bait includes fish and worms.

Availability: Whole, dressed, fillets; fresh and frozen.

Nutritive Value: High in protein, thiamine and niacin.

Best Ways To Serve It: Fried, boiled, steamed or poached.

COBIA

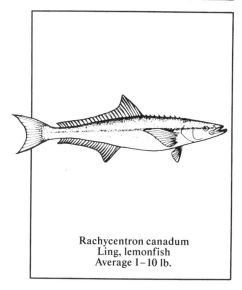

COBIA

Rachycentron canadum
Ling, lemonfish
Average 1–10 lb.

About The Cobia: A popular sport fish, the cobia is sometimes mistaken for a shark because of its size and because it is usually sighted close to shore near the water's surface. The cobia is brown with a black band running along its side. It usually travels alone or in very small groups.

Where It's Caught: In all tropical waters and in the Atlantic from Cape Cod to Argentina. The cobia is usually found around wrecks, reefs or buoys.

When It's Caught: March through November. The best fishing is from May through September.

How It's Caught: Bottom fishing, live lining or casting from shore; trolling from boats. Baits include mullet, squid, live fish and artificial lures.

Availability: Whole, dressed, fillets; fresh and frozen..

Nutritive Value: High in protein.

Best Ways To Serve It: Baked or broiled.

COD

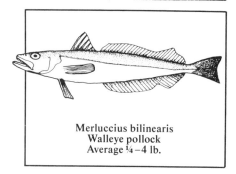

WHITING

Merluccius bilinearis
Walleye pollock
Average ¼–4 lb.

About The Whiting: A member of the cod family, the whiting wasn't considered at all important until about 1920, when it first began to appear in fried fish shops in Missouri. The silvery iridescent whiting is a voracious eater, and will sometimes swim ashore in pursuit of its prey. It eats the young of other species, as well as squid and crustaceans.

Where It's Caught: On the Atlantic continental shelf from Newfoundland to Cape Hatteras. Its habitat ranges from very shallow water to depths of more than 3,000 feet. Since it prefers relatively warm weather, it migrates south in the winter.

When It's Caught: May through October.

How It's Caught: Lines from shore or boats. Baits include cut fish, squid and artificial lures. Commercial fishing vessels catch whiting with otter trawls.

Availability: Whole, fillets; fresh and frozen; frozen portions.

Nutritive Value: High in protein.

Best Ways To Serve It: Baked, broiled, pan-fried, steamed or poached.

DOLPHIN

About The Dolphin:

The dolphin is an exceptionally beautiful game fish whose green and golden coloring becomes brighter and more intense when the fish is feeding or especially alert. It is unrelated to the mammal of the same name. The fish is strong and repeatedly leaps out of the water when hooked. It lives for only three to four years, but during that time it may gain five pounds per month. Although most dolphins are small, weighing two to five pounds, they are capable of reaching weights up to 40 or 50 pounds. The largest ever recorded was an 85-pounder caught off the Bahamas. The dolphin is primarily available in Hawaii under the name "mahi mahi."

Where It's Caught:
In all tropical and subtropical waters. The dolphin moves northward with the warm currents from the Gulf Stream and is abundant from North Carolina to Florida, throughout the Caribbean to Brazil, and from southern California down the South American coast.

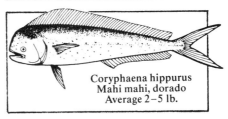

Coryphaena hippurus
Mahi mahi, dorado
Average 2–5 lb.

The dolphin is found near the surface in waters warmer than 70° F.

When It's Caught:
Late April through November.

How It's Caught:
Trolling or casting from boats. Because the swift-moving fish is not easily netted, even commercial vessels have to depend on hooks or lines for their catch. Baits include whole mullet, squid, Spanish mackerel.

Availability:
Whole, dressed, fillets; fresh and frozen.

Nutritive Value:
High in protein.

Best Ways To Serve It:
Baked, broiled, pan-fried or poached.

DRUM

About The Weakfish:
The weakfish was listed on the menu at historical Fraunces Tavern in New York under its original Indian name, squeateague, during George Washington's tenure as United States President. Its present name refers not to a lack of strength but to the delicate tissues around the weakfish's mouth, which are easily torn when the fish is hooked. It is a popular and abundant game fish.

Where It's Caught:
Along the Atlantic coast from Massachusetts to the east coast of Florida. The weakfish is found in the sea, in inlets, bays, channels and creeks, but does not enter fresh waters. It prefers shallow, sandy-bottom areas.

When It's Caught:
April through July.

How It's Caught:
Lines from

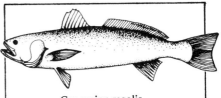

Cynoscion regalis
Gray weakfish, squeateague, yellowfin
Average 2–5 lb.

boats and shore. Baits include worms, shrimp, squid, crabs, live fish and artificial lures. Commercial vessels use nets.

Availability:
Whole, dressed, fillets; fresh and frozen.

Nutritive Value:
High in protein, thiamine and niacin.

Best Ways To Serve It:
Broiled or baked.

59

FLOUNDER

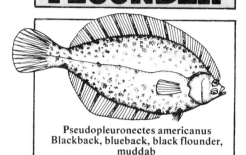

WINTER FLOUNDER

Pseudopleuronectes americanus
Blackback, blueback, black flounder,
muddab
Average 1–2 lb.

About The Winter Flounder:

The winter flounder is one of the best-known and most commercially valuable Eastern flatfish. Its coloring ranges from reddish brown to a deep gray-black, some-times with deep green markings. The winter flounder is prized for its sweet, finely textured white meat.

Where It's Caught: Down the Atlantic coast from Newfoundland to the Chesapeake Bay. The winter flounder prefers shallow water, but is sometimes found in depths up to 400 feet. It tends to move into shallow water in the fall and back into deep water in the spring.

When It's Caught: From November through May. The best fishing is in March and April.

How It's Caught: Lines from anchored or drifting boats. Baits include cut fish and artificial lures.

Availability: Fillets; fresh and frozen.

Nutritive Value: High in protein, thiamine and niacin.

Best Ways To Serve It: Fried, sautéed or broiled.

GREENLING

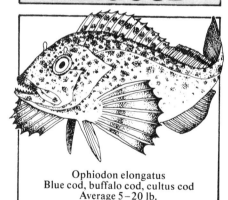

LINGCOD

Ophiodon elongatus
Blue cod, buffalo cod, cultus cod
Average 5–20 lb.

About The Lingcod:

Although its name implies that it belongs to the cod family, the lingcod is a member of the *hexagrammidae* family, a species commonly known as greenlings. The brown or bluish-green lingcod is native to the Pacific and occasionally reaches weights up to 100 pounds.

Where It's Caught: From California's Baja Peninsula to northwest Alaska, in depths of 360 to 600 feet. The lingcod is a bottom dweller and prefers to live near reefs and kelp beds.

When It's Caught: Year round.

How It's Caught: Nearly all lingcod caught are harvested by commercial vessels, using otter trawls, set lines, hand lines and troll lines.

Availability: Dressed, fillets, steaks; fresh and frozen.

Nutritive Value: High in protein and thiamine.

Best Ways To Serve It: Broiled, poached or pan-fried.

SEA TROUT

About The Silver Sea Trout: The silver sea trout is a saltwater fish. It is a uniform pale silvery color and has no distinguishing marks, although some fish do have faint dark spots.

Where It's Caught: Along the Atlantic coast from Maryland to Florida and throughout the Gulf of Mexico. The silver sea trout is usually found in depths of about 60 feet. It prefers to live on sandy bottoms, but can be found in rocky areas as well.

When It's Caught: March through December. The best fishing is in June and July.

How It's Caught: Bottom fishing and live lining from shore; trolling from boats. Baits include shrimp, squid, clams, cut fish and artificial lures.

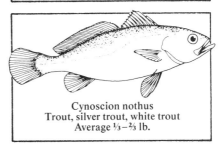

SILVER SEA TROUT

Cynoscion nothus
Trout, silver trout, white trout
Average ⅓–⅔ lb.

Availability: Whole, dressed, fillets; fresh and frozen.
Nutritive Value: High in protein.
Best Ways To Serve It: Broiled, fried or sautéed.

About The Spotted Sea Trout: The spotted sea trout is one of the most popular saltwater game fish in the southern United States. Its upper body is dark gray with pale blue iridescent patches; the lower part is silvery. The spotted sea trout takes its name from the dark round spots on its sides.

Where It's Caught: Along the Atlantic coast from New York to Florida, and in the Gulf of Mexico. The spotted sea trout prefers water temperatures above 50°F.

When It's Caught: Mid–May through early December. The best fishing is from late July through early November.

How It's Caught: Lines from shore; trolling from boats. Baits include shrimp, silversides, mullet, killifish and soft crab. Artificial lures are also effective.

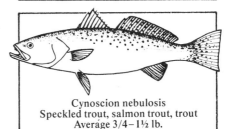

SPOTTED SEA TROUT

Cynoscion nebulosis
Speckled trout, salmon trout, trout
Average 3/4–1½ lb.

Availability: Whole, drawn, fillets; fresh and frozen.
Nutritive Value: High in protein and vitamin A.
Best Ways To Serve It: Fried or sautéed.

SNAPPER

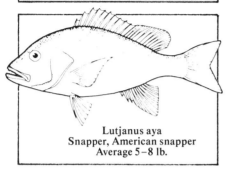

RED SNAPPER

Lutjanus aya
Snapper, American snapper
Average 5–8 lb.

tinctive rosy red in color, and its eyes are bright red.

Where It's Caught: In the middle Atlantic and Gulf coasts from North Carolina to Brazil. Red snapper is especially abundant off the coast of Florida.

When It's Caught: Year round in depths of 150 feet or more; during the warm months in shallower waters.

How It's Caught: Bottom fishing from anchored or drifting boats. Baits include squid, cut fish, shrimp and clams.

Availability: All forms, fresh and frozen.

Nutritive Value: High in protein, low in fat.

About The Red Snapper:
The red snapper is the best-known of all snappers, and has a reputation as an excellent eating fish. It is a dis-

Best Ways To Serve It: Lends itself to all preparation methods, but is especially good stuffed and baked.

LIGHT MEAT/LIGHT FLAVOR

DRUM

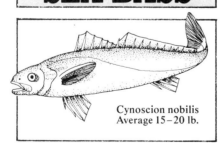

WHITE SEA BASS

Cynoscion nobilis
Average 15–20 lb.

The white sea bass' coloring ranges from pale blue to black, with a white belly and silver iridescence on its sides.

Where It's Caught: In the Pacific, primarily along the coast from San Francisco to Chile. It is usually found near kelp beds.

When It's Caught: May through September.

How It's Caught: Lines from anchored boats; trolling. Baits include live small fish and worms and artificial lures.

Availability: The white sea bass is usually found in California as steaks or fillets; fresh and frozen.

Nutritive Value: High in protein, thiamine and niacin.

About The White Sea Bass: Despite its name, the white sea bass is a member of the drum, not the bass, family. It is closely related to the East coast's weakfish.

Best Ways To Serve It:
Broiled, poached or baked.

GROUPER

About The Black Grouper:

The term "grouper" refers not to a specific fish but to a type of fish belonging to the sea bass family. Groupers are prized for their eating qualities. Because they live near reefs and outcroppings and must be caught with lines and hooks instead of nets, they're not abundant commercially and are therefore considered even more valuable.

Where It's Caught: Off the Florida coast and throughout the south Atlantic to Brazil. Smaller fish may be found near the shore; larger, older fish are usually found further out to sea.

When It's Caught: Year round.

How It's Caught: Trolling with natural bait or artificial lures.

Availability: Fillets; fresh and frozen.

Nutritive Value: High in protein.

Best Ways To Serve It: Baked or fried.

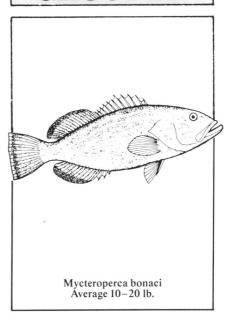

BLACK GROUPER

Mycteroperca bonaci
Average 10–20 lb.

About The Gag Grouper:

Although the gag grouper is not quite as tasty as some other groupers, it is commercially important.

Where It's Caught: In the southern Atlantic from North Carolina to Florida and in the Gulf of Mexico westward to Louisiana. The gag grouper is usually found in water deeper than 60 feet.

When It's Caught: Year round.

How It's Caught: Bottom fishing from anchored boats. Baits include shrimp, squid, clams, cut and live fish and artificial lures.

Availability: Whole, dressed, fillets; fresh and frozen

Nutritive Value: High in protein and thiamine.

Best Ways To Serve It: Baked.

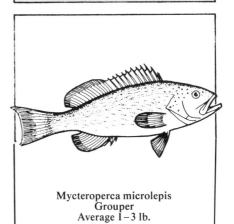

GAG GROUPER

Mycteroperca microlepis
Grouper
Average 1–3 lb.

NASSAU GROUPER

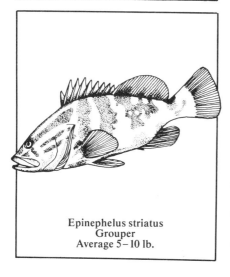

Epinephelus striatus
Grouper
Average 5–10 lb.

About The Nassau Grouper: One of the most well-known groupers, the Nassau grouper is the major commercial fish of the West Indies.

Where It's Caught: Throughout the southern Atlantic. The Nassau grouper is probably so named because it is extremely abundant near the Bahamas. It prefers to live near rocky bottoms in shallow waters.

When It's Caught: Year round.

How It's Caught: Bottom fishing from boats and shore. Baits include shrimp, squid, live and cut fish and artificial lures.

Availability: Whole, dressed, fillets; fresh and frozen.

Nutritive Value: High in protein.

Best Ways To Serve It: Baked or fried; in chowders.

RED GROUPER

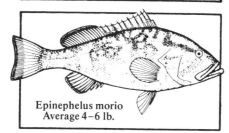

Epinephelus morio
Average 4–6 lb.

About The Red Grouper: The red grouper is a member of the sea bass family (see black grouper).

Where It's Caught: Off southern Florida and in tropical Atlantic waters. It is found near rock and coral outcroppings in depths up to 900 feet.

When It's Caught: Year round.

How It's Caught: Bottom fishing from anchored or drifting boats. Baits include squid, shrimp, cut and live fish and artificial lures.

Availability: Fillets; fresh and frozen.

Nutritive Value: High in protein.

Best Ways To Serve It: Baked or fried.

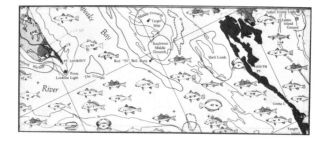

About The Warsaw
Grouper: One of the largest of all groupers, the warsaw grouper occasionally reaches weights of up to 500 pounds. It is sometimes mistakenly called a black grouper because of its coloring.

Where It's Caught: In the Southern Atlantic, from Virginia to southern Florida. The warsaw grouper is sometimes found in depths of 200 feet or more and prefers to live near rocky or coral-covered bottoms.

When It's Caught: Year round in depths of more than 120 feet; during the summer months in depths of more than 60 feet.

How It's Caught: Bottom fishing or trolling from boats. Baits include squid, cut fish, shrimps, crabs, live fish and artificial lures.

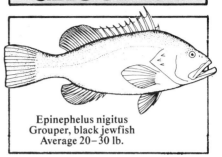

Epinephelus nigitus
Grouper, black jewfish
Average 20–30 lb.

Availability: Fillets, steaks; fresh and frozen.
Nutritive Value: High in protein and thiamine.
Best Ways To Serve It:
Baked or in chunks in chowders.

About The Yellowfin
Grouper: The yellowfin grouper is distinguished by the dark spots on its body. The fins on its sides are rimmed with yellow.

Where It's Caught: Throughout the south Atlantic, especially near Florida. It is usually found near rocky bottoms.

When It's Caught: Year round.
How It's Caught: Bottom fishing from shore or boats. Baits include cut fish, live fish and artificial lures.

Availability: Whole, dressed, fillets; fresh and frozen.
Nutritive Value: High in protein.
Best Ways To Serve It:
Baked, broiled or fried.

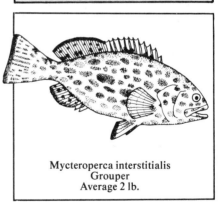

Mycteroperca interstitialis
Grouper
Average 2 lb.

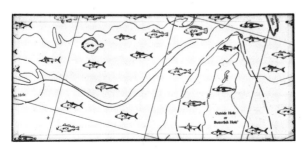

PERCH

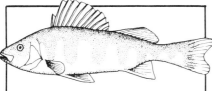

YELLOW PERCH

Perca flavescens
Striped perch, coon perch, jack perch
Average ½ lb.

About The Yellow Perch:
The yellow perch is a close relative of the European perch. The similarities between the two are so great that some experts believe they may belong to the same species. Both are abundant and renowned for their excellent eating qualities. The perch is a favorite with sport fishermen.

Where It's Caught: In lakes in Kansas, Missouri, Illinois, Indiana, Ohio, Carolina and Florida, and in the Great Lakes.

When It's Caught: Year round.

How It's Caught: Perch don't require any sophisticated reels, baits or artificial lures — any line, hook and bait will do.

Availability: Whole; fresh and frozen.

Nutritive Value: High in protein, thiamine and niacin.

Best Ways To Serve It: Pan-fried.

SEA BASS

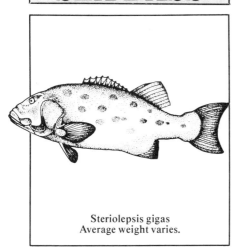

GIANT SEA BASS

Steriolepsis gigas
Average weight varies.

About The Giant Sea Bass:
One of the largest of all bass, the giant sea bass is sometimes mistakenly called black sea bass or jewfish, two species to which it is unrelated. It has been documented at weights up to 550 pounds, but fish of that size are unusual. Those caught by sport fishermen range from five to 100 pounds.

Where It's Caught: In the Pacific off central California south to the Gulf of California off Mexico. Most giant sea bass are caught relatively close to shore.

When It's Caught: Year round, in small numbers.

How It's Caught: Lines from boats.

Availability: The giant sea bass is not widely available commercially, but is sometimes marketed as steaks and fillets; fresh and frozen.

Nutritive Value: High in protein.

Best Ways To Serve It: Baked or broiled.

SMELT

About The Smelt: The smelt takes its name from the ancient Anglo-Saxon word "smoelt," meaning smooth and shining. This slender silver fish is a distant relative of the salmon family.

Where It's Caught: Smelt are plentiful along the north Atlantic and Pacific coasts, in the Columbia River and in bays from Mexico to Canada. It is especially abundant in the Great Lakes. Smelt are found near the surface of the water and as deep as 30 feet below the surface.

When It's Caught: Year round. Sport fishermen should check local laws governing fishing seasons.

How It's Caught: Lines from shore or boats. Baits include shrimp, cut fish and worms. Commercial

SMELT

Osmerus mordax
Whitebait, grunion, jacksmelt
Average 1–4 oz. (more than 10 oz.
is unusual)

vessels use gill nets and trap nets.

Availability: Whole, dressed, breaded, precooked; fresh and frozen.

Nutritive Value: Lean meat, very high in protein.

Best Ways to Serve It: Baked or broiled.

STURGEON

About The Lake Sturgeon: Sometimes referred to as "living fossil" the lake sturgeon has evolved very little since prehistoric times. Instead of scales, the fish has bony, dinosaur-like plates. Lake sturgeon, like all members of the sturgeon family, are slow-growing, and do not reach maturity until the ages of 12 to 22. A five-year-old lake sturgeon may weigh only two pounds, but a fully mature sturgeon may weigh 20 to 30 pounds. Some sturgeon live up to 80 years. Other members of the sturgeon family include the Atlantic sturgeon, green sturgeon, pallid sturgeon, shortnose sturgeon, shovelnose sturgeon and white sturgeon. The white sturgeon is the largest of the family — one reportedly weighed in at 1,800 pounds.

Where It's Caught: In lakes and streams from the Hudson Bay to the St. Lawrence River in Canada, and throughout Minnesota, Nebras-

LAKE STURGEON

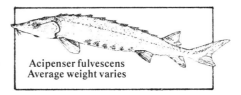

Acipenser fulvescens
Average weight varies

ka, Missouri, northern Alabama, and in the Great Lakes.

When It's Caught: April through June.

How It's Caught: Lines from boats and shore. Baits include cut fish.

Availability: Whole, steaks, chunks; fresh and frozen.

Nutritive Value: Fatty flesh, but high in protein.

Best Ways To Serve It: Baked or broiled.

SUNFISH

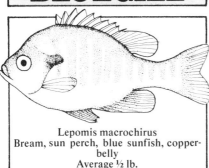

BLUEGILL

Lepomis macrochirus
Bream, sun perch, blue sunfish, copper-belly
Average ½ lb.

About The Bluegill: The most well-known of all sunfish, the freshwater bluegill is one of North America's most popular panfish. The bluegill's body is a variety of colors—it can range from yellow to dark blue, with a large black patch on the back of its top fin.

Where It's Caught: Native to Minnesota, the Great Lakes region, Arkansas and the southeast, bluegills have been introduced to and are thriving in ponds in nearly every state. They prefer to live in weedy areas or underneath docks.

When It's Caught: Year round.

How It's Caught: Lines from shore and boats. Baits include cut fish, worms and artificial lures.

Availability: Whole, dressed, fillets; fresh and frozen.

Nutritive Value: High in protein.

Best Ways To Serve It: Pan-fried or deep-fried.

WHITE CRAPPIE

Pomoxis annularis
Specked perch, bachelor perch, calico bass, papermouth
Average 1 lb.

About The White Crappie: A member of the sunfish family, the white crappie is a popular game fish. The white crappie population is cyclic—it is abundant for several years, then scarce for several years. This is due to the presence of a "dominant brood"—the offspring of a particular year when conditions are optimal and there is an abundance of large, healthy fish that eat their own young and weaker fish. The dominant brood continue to eliminate the young until most of the dominant fish have died or been caught, and the young then have a chance to grow to maturity. Eventually, another dominant brood appears and the cycle repeats itself.

Where It's Caught: In rivers and lakes from Lake Ontario westward to Nebraska, through Ohio and Mississippi, southward to Texas and Alabama, northward to North Carolina, and in California.

When It's Caught: Year round.

How It's Caught: Lines from boats and shore. Baits include shrimp and cut fish.

Availability: Whole, dressed, fillets; fresh and frozen.

Nutritive Value: High in protein.

Best Ways To Serve It: Pan-fried, baked or broiled.

TROUT

About The Brook Trout:

The brook trout is generally considered to have the best eating qualities of all trout. It is characterized by its bright coloring — its sides are covered with blue spots with red centers, dark wavy lines and pink fins. It is very popular with sport fishermen and is considered the principal game fish in parts of New England.

Where It's Caught: In lakes and streams throughout the northeastern United States, and in the Great Lakes.

When It's Caught: September through December.

How It's Caught: Casting from boats and shore. Baits include cut fish and artificial lures.

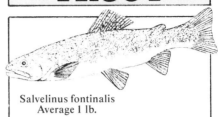

Salvelinus fontinalis
Average 1 lb.

Availability: Whole; fresh and frozen.

Nutritive Value: High in protein.

Best Ways To Serve It: Fried, sautéed or baked.

About The Rainbow Trout:

A popular game fish, the rainbow trout is noted for the vigorous leaps and runs it makes when hooked. It takes its name from the broad reddish band that runs along its side from head to tail. The band blends into the olive-green color of its back and the silver of its belly. Its entire body is spotted with black. The brightness of the rainbow trout varies according to the fish's habitat and diet. Some rainbow trout migrate to the ocean to spawn, and the salt water gives them a grayish tinge. These fish are called steelheads.

Where It's Caught: The rainbow trout is native to cold lakes along the Pacific slope of the Sierras from Alaska to California. It has been introduced in nearly every state in the country. It thrives only in unpolluted waters.

When It's Caught: Some are caught year round, but most are harvested from January through June.

How It's Caught: Casting from boats and shore. Baits include cut

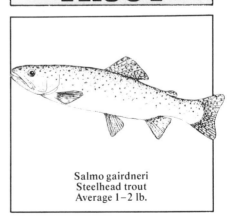

Salmo gairdneri
Steelhead trout
Average 1–2 lb.

fish and artificial lures. Trout are farmed for commercial consumption.

Availability: Whole, boned; fresh and frozen.

Nutritive Value: High in protein, thiamin and niacin.

Best Ways To Serve It: Fried, sautéed or broiled.

69

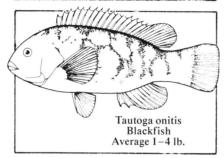

TAUTOG

Tautoga onitis
Blackfish
Average 1–4 lb.

About The Tautog: A member of the wrasse family, the tautog has a gray or greenish-colored body. It has a rounded head and unusually thick lips.
Where It's Caught: Although the tautog is found from Nova Scotia to South Carolina, it is abundant only between Cape Cod and the Delaware Bay. A bottom dweller, the tautog is nearly always found in water less than 60 feet deep. It prefers to live near rocky coastal areas, or near shellfish beds, wrecks and pilings.
When It's Caught: Year round, although the best fishing is in May, June, September and October.
How It's Caught: Bottom fishing from shore or anchored boats.
Availability: Most tautog are eaten by sport fishermen. They are not usually commercially available,
Nutritive Value: High protein.
Best Ways To Serve It: Broiled or baked.

 LIGHT MEAT/MODERATE FLAVOR

BASS

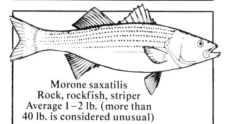

STRIPED SEA BASS

Morone saxatilis
Rock, rockfish, striper
Average 1–2 lb. (more than 40 lb. is considered unusual)

About The Striped Sea Bass: The striped bass was a vital part of the fishery resource for the early American colonists. Historians of that era described the striped bass as the "boldest, bravest, strongest and most active fish that visited the tidal waters and bays along the Atlantic seaboard." It was one of the first fish to be protected under a conservation law enacted in 1639. Today both recreational and commercial fishermen consider it one of the most valuable and popular fish available.

Where It's Caught: Striped sea bass are native to the Atlantic coast of North America. They range from the St. Lawrence River to northern Florida, and may also be found in streams along the Gulf of Mexico from western Florida to Louisiana. They are abundant in the Chesapeake Bay and the Albermarle Sound. In the late 1800's, they were introduced on the Pacific coast and now range from San Diego to Oregon.
When It's Caught: The striped sea bass can be found throughout the year, but the best fishing is in mid-March, May through September, and December.
How It's Caught: Casting, bottom fishing, and trolling. Baits include worms, clams, crab, shrimp, eel and live baitfish, in addition to imitation eel and worms.
Availability: Filleted, steaks, chunks; whole, dressed; fresh and frozen.
Nutritive Value: High in protein.
Best Ways To Serve It: Boiled, steamed and poached.

About The White Perch: The white perch is used as the symbol of the Schuylkill Fishing Company in Pennsylvania, a fishing and sporting club that has been in existence since before the American Revolution. The company's original flag depicted a crown and three white perch, signifying the perch's importance to the early Americans. The white perch was so plentiful and popular that it was served at all the Company's meetings and is still featured at the organization's gatherings.

Where It's Caught: In fresh and salt water from Nova Scotia to North Carolina and inland as far as the Great Lakes.

When It's Caught: May through July.

How It's Caught: Lines from shore and boats. Baits include cut fish, worms, clams and artificial lures.

Availability: Whole, dressed; fresh and frozen.

Nutritive Value: High in protein.

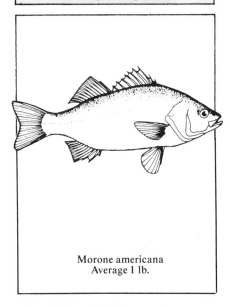

WHITE PERCH

Morone americana
Average 1 lb.

Best Ways To Serve It: Pan-fried, oven-fried or poached.

COD

About The Burbot: The burbot is the only freshwater member of the cod family found in North America. It is an unattractive fish, resembling a misshapen eel with a thick, olive-colored skin. The burbot often has a chain of black or yellow markings running along its sides.

Where It's Caught: The burbot prefers cold, deep waters and has been caught in depths up to 700 feet. It is found in New England and the Susquehanna River, the Great Lakes and the Columbia River.

When It's Caught: Year round.

How It's Caught: Bottom fishing from anchored or drifting boats. Baits include clams, worms and cut fish.

Availability: Whole, dressed, fillets; fresh and frozen. Burbot liver and roe are also considered good to eat.

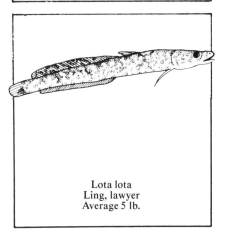

BURBOT

Lota lota
Ling, lawyer
Average 5 lb.

Nutritive Value: High in protein and riboflavin.

Best Ways To Serve It: Broiled, baked or poached.

POLLOCK

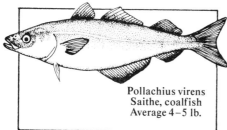

Pollachius virens
Saithe, coalfish
Average 4–5 lb.

About The Pollock: A member of the cod family, the pollock looks very much like a cod, with a more rounded body and forked tail. The pollock is especially popular with recreational fishermen because it is found in shallower water than most other cod, and occasionally reaches weights up to 35 pounds.

Where It's Caught: In the Atlantic ocean, from Newfoundland to the Chesapeake Bay. Off the coast of Europe, the pollock is caught from the North Sea to the Bay of Biscay. It is found close to the shoreline, along sandy and gravel-covered bottoms.

When It's Caught: Year round. The best fishing is from December through March.

How It's Caught: Live lining or bottom fishing from shore. Baits include worms, cut fish, clams and artificial lures.

Availability: Whole, dressed, fillets; fresh and frozen.

Nutritive Value: High in protein and riboflavin.

Best Ways To Serve It: Boiled, steamed or poached.

DRUM

ATLANTIC CROAKER

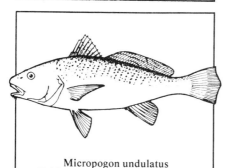

Micropogon undulatus
Golden croaker, croaker, hardhead
Average ¼ – ⅓ lb.

About The Atlantic Croaker: The Atlantic croaker is a pale silver gray with a pattern of broken darker bars across its back, making it appear somewhat spotted. During the spawning season its color changes to yellow or bronze and it is then sometimes know as the "golden croaker."

Where It's Caught: Along the Atlantic coast from Rhode Island to Cape Kennedy, and in the Gulf of Mexico. Atlantic croakers are bottom feeders and are found around rock outcroppings. Young croakers are born offshore in depths up to 300 feet and migrate inshore toward shallower waters. After their first year, they move seaward, migrating again toward shore in the spring and returning to sea in the fall.

When It's Caught: Mid-April through late November. Atlantic croakers are most plentiful in August and September.

How It's Caught: Lines from shore or boats. Baits include clams, worms and cut fish.

Availability: Pan-dressed, fresh and frozen; frozen portions.

Nutritive Value: The lean white meat contains about 17 percent protein.

Best Ways To Serve It: Fried, sautéed, and broiled.

About The Black Drum: The large black drum is of primary commercial value in the Carolinas, where it is popularly used in chowders. The fish's name is misleading, since it is not black but silver with a bronze sheen. Its fins are dark grey or black. Its throat contains large, powerful teeth, which it uses to crush shellfish.

Where It's Caught: It is abundant from Cape Cod to Argentina, especially from Virginia to the northern Gulf of Mexico. The black drum is a bottom feeder.

When It's Caught: April through mid-November. Small fish are caught from September through early November; large fish are caught in May and June.

How It's Caught: Bottom fishing from shore or boats land large fish; the same methods used with artificial lures attract small fish. Commercial vessels use long lines and trammel nets.

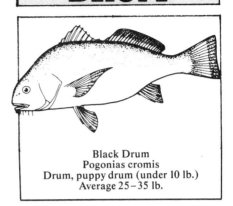

Black Drum
Pogonias cromis
Drum, puppy drum (under 10 lb.)
Average 25–35 lb.

Availability: Whole, dressed, fillets; fresh and frozen.
Nutritive Value: High in protein.
Best Ways To Serve It: Baked, broiled, steamed or poached.

About The Spot: A member of the croaker family, spot are also identified by two other names — small spot caught in the spring are called "white eyes," and large spot caught in the fall are called "yellowfins." Like all croakers, male spot make a drumming sound. Both male and female spot are bluish-gray with a golden iridescence near the spine.

Where It's Caught: Along the Atlantic coast from Cape Cod into the Gulf of Mexico. Spot are most abundant south of New Jersey.

When It's Caught: Late April through mid-December. Large spot are caught in September and November.

How It's Caught: Bottom fishing from shore; trolling from boats. Baits include shrimp, worms, clams and cut fish.

Availability: Pan-dressed, fresh and frozen.

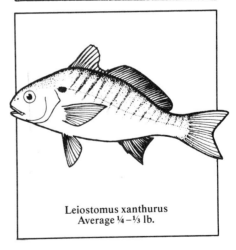

Leiostomus xanthurus
Average ¼–⅓ lb.

Nutritive Value: High in protein and riboflavin.
Best Ways To Serve It: Pan-fried.

EEL

Anguilla rostrata
Average 1½–2 lb.

About The Eel: Although highly prized in most European nations, the eel is regarded somewhat suspiciously by most Americans. It is one of the most mysterious fish — man speculated on its origins for 23 centuries until, in 1924, its true habits were revealed to be more fantastic than most of the myths surrounding it. North American eels are born in the Sargasso Sea, in the southwest part of the North Atlantic. Baby eels, known as elvers, travel for over a year before reaching the North American coast: they arrive at the shores in the spring. When fully mature, they head back out to sea, to a spawning ground located south of Bermuda and 1,000 miles east of Florida. Once there, the North American eels meet European eels, who have journeyed to the same place. Although their breeding grounds overlap, the offspring of North American eels always return to North America, while the offspring of European eels always return to Europe.

Where It's Caught: Eels are found along the bottom of ponds and rivers and near the shore of the North Atlantic coast.

When It's Caught: Late March through December.

How It's Caught: Bottom fishing from shore using any natural bait.

Availability: Whole, fillets; fresh and frozen.

Nutritive Value: High in protein and vitamin A.

Best Ways To Serve It: Fried, sautéed, baked.

MULLETS

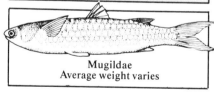

Mugildae
Average weight varies

About The Mullet: The mullet is not one fish but a family of many, all of which are abundant and nutritious. In fact, the United States supply of mullet has traditionally exceeded the demand for it. The best-known and probably most popular "mullet" is the European red mullet, which, in fact, is not a mullet but a member of the goatfish family. There are approximately six species of mullet found in North American waters. Of these, the striped and silver mullet are the most abundant and commercially important. The striped mullet has a bluish-gray or green upper body and a silver lower body. Its scales have dark centers, forming lines that run down the sides of the mullet's body. The striped mullet can weigh more than 15 pounds. The silver mullet (sometimes known as "white mullet") has a silvery body without any distinguising marks. It rarely weighs more than two pounds.

Where It's Caught: The striped mullet is found along the East coast from Cape Cod to Brazil. The silver mullet has a similar range.

When It's Caught: The striped mullet is caught from November through March; the silver mullet is caught from April through July.

How It's Caught: Bottom fishing from boats and shore.

Availability: Whole, dressed, fillets; fresh and frozen.

Nutritive Value: High in protein, thiamine, niacin and vitamin A.

Best Ways To Serve It: Broiled, fried or sautéed.

PIKE

About The Northern Pike:

The northern pike appears to be elongated and somewhat flattened. Its head is large, with very pointed teeth. The northern pike's popularity as food has fluctuated over the centuries. In 1653, in *The Compleat Angler*, Izaak Walton called the pike "choicely good" and gave eleborate instructions on how it should be prepared. However, there is evidence that American Indians had no use for pike, and even today the Dogrib and Cree tribes use it only as dog food.

Where It's Caught:

The northern pike is most common in the fresh waters of New York through the Great Lakes region to Nebraska, although it has also been introduced into many northern and western states.

When It's Caught:

Spring and summer, usually during daylight hours.

How It's Caught:

Lines from boats. Baits include cut fish and shrimp.

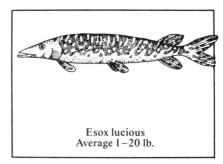

Esox lucious
Average 1–20 lb.

Availability:

Whole, dressed, fillets and steaks; fresh and frozen.

Nutritive Value:

Lean flesh that's high in protein.

Best Ways To Serve It:

Fried, sautéed or baked.

POMPANO

About The Pompano:

The pompano has several extremely unusual habits — it can appear to walk rapidly over the surface of the water, skim along the surface on its side like a skipping stone, or leap out of shallow water and streak through the air. It is not uncommon for the pompano to throw itself onto the deck of a boat. The small silver fish is highly prized as food, and tends to be very expensive.

Where It's Caught:

The pompano can be found from Massachusetts to Brazil. It is abundant in the Atlantic from North Carolina to Florida, and in the Gulf of Mexico.

When It's Caught:

April through early December.

How It's Caught:

Bottom fishing and casting from shore; trolling from boats. Baits include shrimp, clams, cut fish and artificial lures.

Availability:

Whole, dressed, fillets; fresh and frozen.

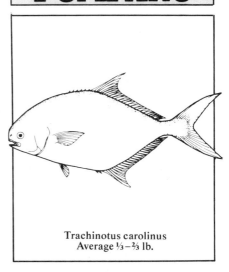

Trachinotus carolinus
Average ⅓–⅔ lb.

Nutritive Value:

High in protein, thiamine and riboflavin.

Best Ways To Serve It:

Baked or broiled.

75

PORGY

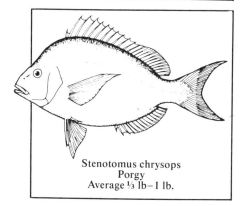

SCUP

Stenotomus chrysops
Porgy
Average ⅓ lb – 1 lb.

About The Scup: The irides-cent, dull-silver scup belongs to the perch family, as do roughly one quarter of the world's 32,000 fresh-and salt-water fish species. All these fish have one distinguishing characteris-tic: the front of their dorsal (top) fin is spiny. Scup are excellent for eating and are popular with recreational and commercial fishermen.

Where It's Caught: Scup live in the coastal waters of the Atlantic from Cape Cod to Cape Hatteras. Young scup can be found in very shallow water, especially during the warm months. They prefer to remain near a smooth, sandy bottom, feeding on the variety of crustaceans that live there. Most are caught in depths of 10 to 90 feet.

When It's Caught: Late May through October.

How It's Caught: Lines and bottom fishing from shore; drifting or anchored boats. Baits include clams, mussels, worms, shrimp, cut fish and live fish.

Availability: Whole, dressed; fresh and frozen.

Nutritive Value: High in protein.

Best Ways To Serve It: Fried, sautéed or baked.

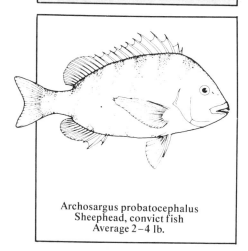

SHEEPSHEAD

Archosargus probatocephalus
Sheephead, convict fish
Average 2 – 4 lb.

About The Sheepshead: A member of the porgy family, this dull-gray fish was once so abundant in waters off New York that it gave Brooklyn's "Sheepshead Bay" its name. It is sometimes called a "con-vict fish" because of the five to seven dark vertical bars that appear on its sides.

Where It's Caught: The sheepshead is found from Nova Scotia to the Gulf of Mexico, but it is abundant only south of the Chesa-peake Bay. It is a bottom dweller most likely to be found near rock jet-ties and bridge abutments.

When It's Caught: The sheeps-head can be caught year round, but the best fishing is from March through October.

How It's Caught: Bottom fish-ing from boats and shore. Baits include crabs, clams, shrimp and artificial lures.

Availability: Whole, dressed, fillets; fresh and frozen.

Nutritive Value: High in protein.

Best Ways To Serve It: Boiled, steamed or poached.

SALMON

About The Atlantic Salmon:
A valuable food and game fish, the Atlantic salmon, like all salmon, is anadromous — capable of living in both fresh and salt water. It is born in fresh water, journeys to the sea as a young fish, and returns at age four or five to its birthplace to spawn. During its journey to the spawning ground, the normally silver-colored Atlantic salmon becomes brownish-red (males) or black (females). Unlike many salmon, Atlantic salmon may spawn more than once.

Where It's Caught: Along the Atlantic coast from Greenland to Cape Cod. It is usually caught when it begins to travel from the ocean into the mouths of streams and rivers.

When It's Caught: Depends upon spawning runs, which vary from year to year and stream to stream. Early runs usually occur from May through June, late runs from July through September.

How It's Caught: Sport fishermen cast from shore and boats, using

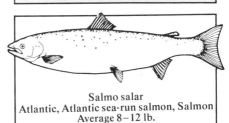

Salmo salar
Atlantic, Atlantic sea-run salmon, Salmon
Average 8–12 lb.

cut fish and artificial lures. Most commercial fishermen string nets in the sea or along the shoreline as salmon migrate to fresh water, but a few troll in the open sea.

Availability: Whole, dressed, chunks, fillets, steaks; fresh, frozen or canned; smoked.

Nutritive Value: High in protein and vitamin A.

Best Ways To Serve It: Fried, sautéed or baked.

About The Chum Salmon:
Less important than other members of the pacific salmon family, the chum salmon was introduced into the Barents Sea by the USSR and is now established in the Soviet Union and Norway. Like most salmon, the chum is born in fresh water, travels downstream to the sea when a few months old and migrates back upstream to its birthplace at age four or five to spawn.

Where It's Caught: From Alaska down the California coast. The chum usually travels to freshwater lakes and streams near the sea.

When It's Caught: November through December, although this can vary according to spawning runs.

How It's Caught: Sport fishermen cast from shore and boats, using cut fish and artificial lures. Most commercial fishermen string nets in

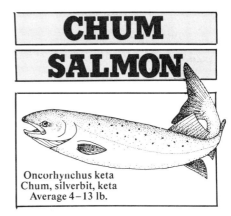

Oncorhynchus keta
Chum, silverbit, keta
Average 4–13 lb.

the sea or along the shoreline as salmon migrate to fresh water.

Availability: Whole, dressed; fresh, frozen and canned; smoked.

Nutritive Value: High in protein and vitamin A.

Best Ways To Serve It:
Baked, broiled, boiled, steamed or poached.

77

CISCO

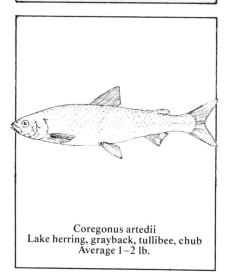

Coregonus artedii
Lake herring, grayback, tullibee, chub
Average 1–2 lb.

About The Cisco: The cisco is often called "lake herring" because it resembles the saltwater herring. In fact, however, it is a member of the salmon family. The cisco has a silvery body, slightly darker on the top than on the sides, and large scales. The North American cisco has no tongue or teeth.

Where It's Caught: In cold-water lakes throughout New England and in the Great Lakes. The cisco can be found from a few feet below the surface to depths of several hundred feet.

When It's Caught: July through November, when it moves inshore to spawn.

How It's Caught: Lines from boats and shore.

Availability: Whole, dressed; fresh and frozen; smoked.

Nutritive Value: High in protein.

Best Ways To Serve It: Fried or sautéed.

COHO SALMON

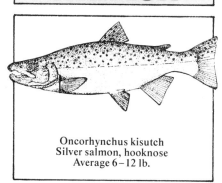

Oncorhynchus kisutch
Silver salmon, hooknose
Average 6–12 lb.

About The Coho Salmon: The coho, like all salmon, can live in both fresh and salt water. Unlike most other salmon, its migrations take place within a fairly small area; it rarely travels more than a few hundred miles from its birthplace. It reaches maturity at age three and begins migration then. The coho salmon is popular with sport fishermen.

Where It's Caught: In the Pacific Ocean from California to Japan, and in the Great Lakes. The coho salmon is also found along the coast of Vancouver Island, Washington and northern California.

When It's Caught: July through February.

How It's Caught: Sport fishermen cast from shore and boats, using cut fish and artificial lures. Most commercial fishermen string nets in the sea or along the shoreline as salmon migrate to fresh water, but a few troll in the open sea. Troll-caught salmon are more valuable because the fish haven't begun migrating and are still eating.

Availability: Whole, dressed, steaks, fillets; fresh and frozen; smoked.

Nutritive Value: High in protein, niacin and vitamin A.

Best Ways To Serve It: Fried, sautéed or poached.

About The Pink Salmon:

The pink salmon is the smallest and most plentiful of all the Pacific salmon, comprising about half of all canned salmon. It is characterized by large oval black spots on its upper back and rear fin. Like most salmon, the pink salmon is born in fresh water, travels downstream to the sea when a few months old and migrates back upstream to its birthplace at age two to spawn.

Where It's Caught:
From Alaska down the California coast. The pink salmon, unlike other salmon, usually spawns in fresh water near the sea.

When It's Caught:
Usually from July through November, although this varies according to spawning runs.

How It's Caught:
Sport fishermen cast from shore and boats, using cut fish and artificial lures. Most commercial fishermen string nets in the sea or along the shoreline as

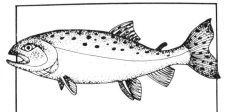

Oncorhynchus gorbusha
Pink, humbpack, humpy
Average 2–6 lb.

salmon migrate to fresh water, but a few troll in the open sea.

Availability:
Whole, dressed; fresh, frozen and canned.

Nutritive Value:
High in protein and vitamin A.

Best Ways To Serve It:
Baked, broiled, boiled, steamed or poached.

SEA BASS

About The Rockfish:
There are more than 50 varieties of rockfish along the West coast of the United States. Many have execellent eating qualities and are popular with commercial and sport fishermen. The most flavorful and commercially important rockfish include the orange, yellowtail, bocaccio and red rockfish. The *orange rockfish* is a light gray fish with yellow-orange stripes that grows to about 30 inches. The *yellowtail rockfish,* a grayish brown fish with dark brown and dusky green patches, takes its name from its yellow fins. The yellowtail grows to about 26 inches. The *bocaccio* is a light green or dark brown fish, washed with clear pale red with deep black spots. "Bocaccio" means "large mouth," this fish's most distingushing characteristic. The bocaccio grows to about 34 inches.

Where It's Caught:
In the north

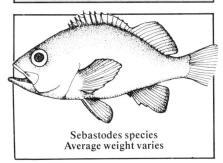

Sebastodes species
Average weight varies

temperate seas from California to Alaska.

When It's Caught:
Year round.

How It's Caught:
Most commercial fishermen use otter trawls.

Availability:
Whole, dressed, fillets; fresh and frozen.

Nutritive Value:
High in protein.

Best Ways To Serve It:
Fried, broiled, or baked.

SKILFISH

SABLEFISH

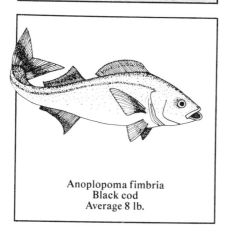

Anoplopoma fimbria
Black cod
Average 8 lb.

About The Sablefish: The sablefish has been an important part of the Pacific coast's fishery resource since the 1890's. Its nickname, "black cod," is misleading, since it is not a member of the cod family. The sablefish gets its name from its black and greenish coloring.

Where It's Caught: From the Bering Sea near Alaska down the California coast. Sablefish are found in shallow coastal waters and in depths of up to 600 fathoms. They are bottom dwellers, and prefer soft mud to rocky areas.

When It's Caught: August through November.

How It's Caught: Lines from boats. Commercial fishing trawlers use modified crab traps.

Availability: Dressed; fresh and frozen; smoked.

Nutritive Value: The fatty flesh is high in vitamin A.

Best Ways To Serve It: Boiled, steamed or poached; especially good in casseroles and salads.

SNAPPER

VERMILLION SNAPPER

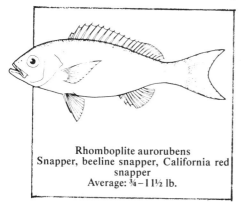

Rhomboplite aurorubens
Snapper, beeline snapper, California red snapper
Average: ¾ – 1 1½ lb.

About The Vermillion Snapper: The vermillion snapper, although tasty, is not noted for excellent eating qualities, as are other snappers. It is red, with pale brown lines running down its spine; yellow lines streak its sides.

Where It's Caught: From the North Carolina coast to Brazil. Vermillion snappers are bottom feeders, and tend to gather on mud, sand, gravel, coral or rocky bottoms in depths of 90 to 350 feet.

When It's Caught: Year round.

How It's Caught: Bottom fishing from anchored or drifting boats. Baits include squid, cut fish, shrimp and clams.

Nutritive Value: High in protein, niacin and phosphorus.

Availability: Whole, fillets; fresh and frozen.

Best Ways To Serve It: Baked or broiled.

SWORDFISH

About The Swordfish: The swordfish is as aggressive as its name and appearance imply. It is not frightened by ships or people and will attack boats that enter its territory with its long, sharp bill. It can ram a boat with enough force to drive the bill deep into a wooden hull. When merchant vessels were sunk off the coast of Bermuda during World War II, bales of rubber frequently washed ashore with swordfish bills embedded in them.

Where It's Caught: Swordfish are found in temperate and tropical oceans throughout the world, in continental shelf waters and in depths of 2,100 feet or more. They prefer to congregate above rock and coral outcroppings.

When It's Caught: Year round. The best fishing is in late winter and early spring.

How It's Caught: Many swordfish are caught by anglers fishing for

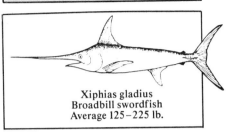

Xiphias gladius
Broadbill swordfish
Average 125–225 lb.

groupers or snappers. Because the fish will boldly approach boats, it is a good candidate for harpooning Most commercially caught swordfish have been harpooned, although some are caught with long lines and others are entangled in tuna nets.

Availability: Steaks, fresh and frozen.

Nutritive Value: High in protein, niacin and vitamin A.

Best Ways To Serve It: Broiled or grilled.

TILEFISH

About The Tilefish: The tilefish is distinguished by its colorful body, which is usually blue or green near its upper back and yellow or rose near its belly. It may be covered with yellow spots, and its fins range from yellow to purple. It is a commercially important fish, with nearly 10 million pounds reaching the marketplace each year. The flavor and texture of its flesh is often compared to that of the lobster.

Where It's Caught: The tilefish prefers extremely deep, cold water, usually between 270 and 1,000 feet. It lives in the Atlantic Ocean from Nova Scotia to Florida, and in the Gulf of Mexico.

When It's Caught: Year round.

How It's Caught: Because they live in such deep water, very few

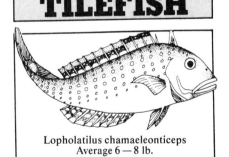

Lopholatilus chamaeleonticeps
Average 6 — 8 lb.

tilefish are caught by sport fishermen. Commercial vessels use nets.

Availability: Whole, dressed, fillets; fresh and frozen.

Nutritive Value: High in protein.

Best Ways To Serve It: Baked or steamed; in salads.

TROUT

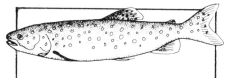

LAKE TROUT

Salvelinus namaycush
Togue, mackinaw, gray trout
Average 10–20 lb.

About The Lake Trout: A member of the salmon family, the lake trout is one of the largest of all trout, reaching weights up to 100 pounds. It is usually bluish-gray or greenish with a bronze sheen, with pale iridescent spots along its sides and fins.

Where It's Caught: In lakes in Alaska and from Maine to Idaho. During cold seasons, when the water is chilled the lake trout may be found near shore; when the weather is warm the fish seeks deep, colder water, often several hundred feet beneath the surface.

When It's Caught: November through May, when it ventures into shallower water.

How It's Caught: Casting and lines from boats. Baits include cut fish and artificial lures.

Availability: Whole, dressed, fillets; fresh and frozen.

Nutritive Value: Fatty flesh that's high in protein.

Best Ways To Serve It: Baked, fried or sautéed.

TUNA

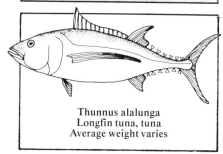

ALBACORE TUNA

Thunnus alalunga
Longfin tuna, tuna
Average weight varies

About The Albacore Tuna: Found in both the Atlantic and Pacific oceans, the albacore tuna has the whitest, most delicately flavored flesh of all tuna and is most important to the commercial fishing industry. Albacore tuna is the only tuna labeled "white meat tuna" when canned.

Where It's Caught: In tropical and temperate waters throughout the Atlantic and Pacific oceans, although most are harvested in the Pacific. The albacore prefers water temperatures of 60° to 66° F. West coast albacore migrate back and forth between Japan and the United States in search of comfortable temperatures. Commercial and recreational fishing vessels travel up to 100 miles offshore in search of tuna.

When It's Caught: From July through October along the West coast.

How It's Caught: Trolling boats use artificial lures to attract a school of fish, then live bait is used to catch it in large quantities. Commercial vessels use purse seine nets.

Availability: Most commercially harvested tuna is canned.

Nutritive Value: Very high in protein.

Best Ways To Serve It: Canned tuna can be eaten plain or mixed with salads or casseroles; tuna steaks can be pan-fried or poached.

About The Bluefin Tuna:

The bluefin tuna is the largest member of the tuna family. Although it is not considered especially valuable in the United States, it is prized in Europe and Japan. Its skin is bluish-green with reflections of green and lavender. It can reach weights up to 1,500 pounds.

Where It's Caught: The bluefin

is found in temperate and subtropical seas. Small fish are found in water warmer than 60° F. Large fish are found in water above 44° F. Bluefin tuna are found both inshore and far out to sea, but rarely in waters less than 20 feet deep.

When It's Caught: Late June

through November.

How It's Caught: Trolling

offshore. Baits include whole squid, mackerel, silver hake or mullet. Chumming can be effective, but this method may attract other kinds of fish as well.

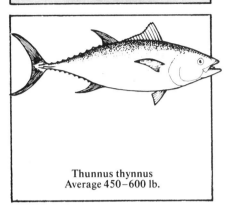

BLUEFIN TUNA

Thunnus thynnus
Average 450–600 lb.

Availability: Canned.
Nutritive Value: High in protein.
Best Ways To Serve It: In any recipe that calls for canned tuna.

About The Yellowfin Tuna:

The yellowfin tuna comprises the bulk of the harvest of the California-based tuna fishing industry. Its meat, when cooked, is neither as light as the albacore nor as dark as the bluefin. It is known as *ahi* in Hawaii and as *shibi* in Japan. The yellowfin is characterized by bright yellow fins and a brilliant yellow stripe along its sides.

Where It's Caught: In tropical

and subtropical waters around the world. It is found as far north as New Jersey when the Gulf Stream sends currents of warm water into the Atlantic.

When It's Caught: Year round

in tropical waters; late spring and summer in cooler waters.

How It's Caught: Enormous

quantities of yellowfin are harvested commercially by vessels using live bait and nets.

Availability: Canned.
Nutritive Value: High in

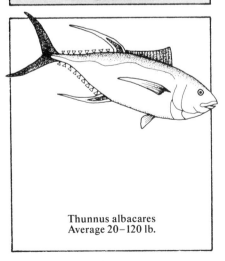

YELLOWFIN TUNA

Thunnus albacares
Average 20–120 lb.

protein.
Best Ways To Serve It: In any recipe that calls for canned tuna.

HERRING

AMERICAN SHAD

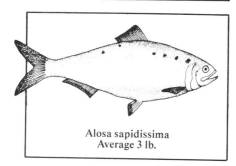

Alosa sapidissima
Average 3 lb.

About The Shad:

The shad is the largest member of the herring family, sometimes reaching weights up to 14 pounds. It was a food staple in the days of the early American settlers. It was so abundant that it became unfashionable among the wealthy, who feared they might be thought unable to afford scarcer, more expensive foods. Its body is silver with a bluish-green iridescense along its upper back. Like the salmon, the shad is born in fresh water, migrates to the sea after about a year, and returns to its natal stream at age four or five to spawn.

Where It's Caught: Along the Atlantic coastline from the St. Lawrence River in Canada to Florida, and in the Gulf of Mexico.

When It's Caught: Shad are caught as they enter streams, from January to June.

How It's Caught: Lines from boats; commercial vessels use nets strung to trap the fish as they migrate to their natural streams.

Availability: Whole, fillets; fresh and frozen. Shad roe, a delicacy, is marketed fresh or canned.

Nutritive Value: High in protein, thiamine and niacin.

Best Ways To Serve It: Broiled, baked or sautéed.

ATLANTIC HERRING

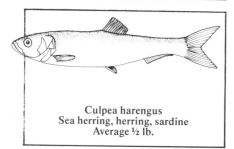

Culpea harengus
Sea herring, herring, sardine
Average ½ lb.

About The Atlantic Herring:

The Atlantic Herring has been an important food at least since the beginning of recorded history. Herring bones have been found in the ruins of homes dating back to 3,000 B.C. Although herring is an important food throughout Europe, it is usually found in the United States only in preserved, cured or pickled form. Immature herring are marketed as sardines.

Where It's Caught: In the Atlantic Ocean from Rhode Island to Maine, in water between 12 and 180 feet deep.

When It's Caught: From July through April.

How It's Caught: Sport fishermen use lines from boats and shore; commercial vessels use pair trawl and purse seine nets.

Availability: Whole, chunks; fresh, salted, pickled and smoked.

Nutritive Value: High in protein.

Best Ways To Serve It: Baked, broiled, fried or sautéed.

About The Maine
Sardine: The word "sardine" refers not to a species of fish but to a group of tiny, soft-boned fish of many species. The word is probably derived from the island of Sardinia in the Mediterranean, where similar fish were first caught in large quantities. The commercially important Maine sardine is actually an immature Atlantic Herring. Its elongated body is greenish blue with a silvery iridescense.

Where It's Caught: Along the Atlantic coast from Greenland to Virginia. The waters off Maine are the center of the sardine industry.

When It's Caught: Sardines are caught at night during the spring, summer and fall months. Their bodies are phosphorescent, so it is easy for fishermen to spot schools.

How It's Caught: Commercial fishermen use stop seines and purse seines. Some use a hose pierced with holes and stretched along the ocean floor. Compressed air pumped through the hose causes bubbles to rise to the surface and, since the fish

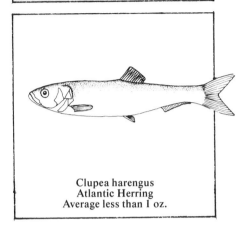

MAINE SARDINE

Clupea harengus
Atlantic Herring
Average less than 1 oz.

will not swim through the bubbles, it is trapped in place.

Availability: Canned.

Nutritive Value: High in protein.

Best Ways To Serve It: In a variety of hors d'oeuvres and snack recipes; straight from the can.

JACK

About The Blue
Runner: This tiny fish is one of the most common species of jack crevalles found in the Atlantic Ocean. The green jack, very similar to the blue runner, is a member of the same family and is found in the Pacific. The blue runner isn't really blue — its body ranges from black to blue-green with dark gray or silver on its belly.

Where It's Caught: Off the coast from Brazil to Nova Scotia, and near the West Indies and Bermuda.

When It's Caught: Year round.

How It's Caught: Lines from boats and shore.

Availability: Whole, dressed, fillets; fresh and frozen.

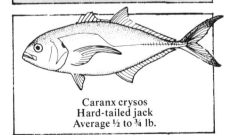

BLUE RUNNER

Caranx crysos
Hard-tailed jack
Average ½ to ¾ lb.

Nutritive Value: High in protein.

Best Ways To Serve It: Pan-fried.

85

MACKEREL

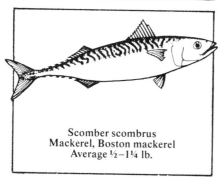

ATLANTIC MACKEREL

Scomber scombrus
Mackerel, Boston mackerel
Average ½–1¼ lb.

About The Atlantic Mackerel: The Atlantic mackerel is distinguished by its brilliant coloring: an iridescent green-blue covers most of the upper body, the head is blue-black and the belly silvery white. It has wavy, darker bands on its upper body. The mackerel belongs to the Scombridae family, the same large family of fish that includes tuna; it sometimes called "wolf of the sea" because it travels in huge, fast-moving schools.

Where It's Caught: The mackerel inhabits the Atlantic coast from Labrador to Cape Hatteras. It is found both offshore and inshore, sometimes even in harbors. It can be found just below the water's surface to depths of 600 feet.

When It's Caught: Mid-May through November.

How It's Caught: Casting from shore. Baits include worms, clams and cut fish.

Availability: Whole, fillets; usually fresh, sometimes frozen or canned.

Nutritive Value: Rich in protein and minerals. The high fat content provides unsaturated fatty acid, useful in reducing serum cholesterol.

Best Ways To Serve It: Broiled or baked.

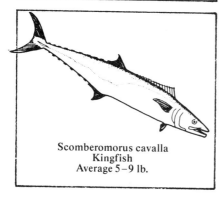

KING MACKEREL

Scomberomorus cavalla
Kingfish
Average 5–9 lb.

About The King Mackerel: The king mackerel, the second-largest member of the mackerel family, reaches weights of up to 100 pounds. Only the wahoo grows larger. The king mackerel is considered an excellent game and eating fish.

Where It's Caught: Off the southern Atlantic coast and in the Gulf of Mexico. The king mackerel is a bottom dweller; it prefers the open ocean and water temperatures above 68° F.

When It's Caught: Mid-June through October.

How It's Caught: Most are caught by boats trolling five to 15 miles offshore; others are caught from shore or piers.

Availability: Drawn, steaks, fillets; fresh and frozen.

Nutritive Value: High in niacin.

Best Ways To Serve It: Baked or broiled.

About The Spanish

Mackerel: The Spanish mackerel is noted for its spectacular leaps out of the water; it reaches heights up to 10 feet above the surface before arching back down into the water. This incredible display, and the fight it offers when hooked, makes the Spanish mackerel especially desirable prey for sport fishermen.

Where It's Caught: Spanish mackerel inhabit both coasts of North America. On the Atlantic coast they are found from Florida to the Chesapeake Bay and occasionally as far north as Cape Cod. On the coast of the Gulf of Mexico, from Florida to Texas, they are far more abundant — they enter bays and sounds in large numbers from May through September. Along the Pacific coast, they range from San Diego to the Galapagos Islands.

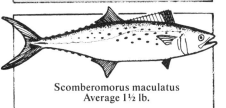

SPANISH MACKEREL

Scomberomorus maculatus
Average 1½ lb.

When It's Caught: Whenever waters are warmer than 67° F.

How It's Caught: Trolling or casting from boats within three miles of the shoreline.

Availability: Whole, dressed, fillets, steaks; fresh and frozen.

Nutritive Value: High in protein, calcium and phosphorus.

Best Ways To Serve It: Broiled or baked.

 ## DARK MEAT/LIGHT TO MODERATE

BLUEFISH

About The Bluefish: Unlike most fish, the bluefish kills far more prey than it consumes and it is not uncommon for it to eat parts of a fish and leave the remains to sink in the sea. It is noted for its "feeding frenzy"—a school of bluefish will attack and kill fish nearly equal their size. Bluefish do not confine their killing to fish of other species—they are cannabalistic as well. Schools of bluefish tend to comprise fish of approximately equal size and strength, so they can defend themselves against one another. Young, small bluefish (called snappers, although they are not related to the snapper species) tend to travel together rather than in a school of fully grown bluefish.

Where It's Caught: The bluefish is found off the Atlantic coast from Cape Cod to Florida. In warm years, it may be found as far north as Nova Scotia. The bluefish prefers temperatures above 55° F. in inlets,

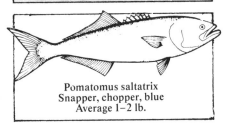

BLUEFISH

Pomatomus saltatrix
Snapper, chopper, blue
Average 1–2 lb.

shoals, near wrecks and inshore reefs.

When It's Caught: Year round, but sport fishing is best in October or November. Fish are harvested commercially in December and January.

How It's Caught: Casting, bottom fishing and lines from shore; trolling form boats.

Availability: Whole, dressed, fillets; fresh and frozen.

Nutritive Value: High in protein, thiamine and niacin.

Best Ways To Serve It: Baked or broiled.

EELPOUT

OCEAN POUT

Ocean Pout
Macozoarces americanus
Yellow eel, congo eel, muttonfish
Average 1½ – 5 lb.

About The Ocean Pout: The ocean pout looks like a cross between a fish and an eel. Unlike an eel, however, it has small fins behind its gills and a large mouth. Its color ranges from dusky yellow to deep brown. The Atlantic-dwelling ocean pout is one of 18 members of the eelpout family, most of whom live in the Pacific Ocean.

Where It's Caught: From the Gulf of St. Lawrence to the Delaware Bay in depths of up to 500 feet.

When It's Caught: During the spring and summer months, when it moves closer to shore. It moves offshore into deeper waters when cold weather begins.

How It's Caught: Lines from boats and shore. Commercial trawlers harvest great numbers of ocean pout, but the fish is still considered underutilized.

Availability: Whole, dressed, fillets; fresh and frozen.

Nutritive Value: High in protein.

Best Ways To Serve It: Fried, poached, boiled or steamed.

SEA BASS

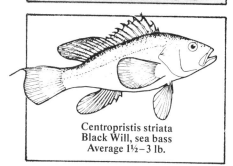

BLACK SEA BASS

Centropristis striata
Black Will, sea bass
Average 1½–3 lb.

About The Black Sea Bass: The black sea bass has been a prize for fishermen since the 18th century. Records show that George Washington once chartered a boat to sail off New York's Sandy Hook banks in search of the small fish. Party-boat fishing for black sea bass was a popular pastime then — posters of fishermen carrying strings of the fish were distributed throughout New York.

Where It's Caught: Black sea bass are found along the Atlantic coast from New York to Carolina. They are migratory, and prefer to live near the ocean bottom and around wrecks, pilings, wharves and jetties. During warm weather they live in depths up to 50 feet; in cold weather they migrate to deeper ocean waters.

When It's Caught: May through October.

How It's Caught: Bottom fishing from drifting or anchored boats; some are caught from shore. Baits include squid, clams, worms and cut fish.

Availability: Whole, fillets; fresh and frozen.

Nutritive Value: High in protein.

Best Ways To Serve It: Broiled, baked, fried or sautéed.

SALMON

About The Chinook Salmon:
The chinook salmon is the largest of the Pacific salmon, reaching weights of more than 100 pounds. Like most salmon, the chinook lives in the sea until it reaches maturity between the ages of one and eight, and travels to fresh water to spawn. It reaches freshwater lakes and streams by swimming against the current in rivers flowing from the fresh water into the sea. Distance appears to be no object to salmon in general, and the chinook travels farther than most — it leaves the sea to enter the Yukon River in the spring bound for spawning streams. Newborn chinook salmon remain in fresh water for at least a year before swimming downstream.

Where It's Caught:
From Alaska to the California coast. Like most salmon, the chinook is usually caught after it has begun its spawning migration.

When It's Caught:
Usually from early spring through the fall.

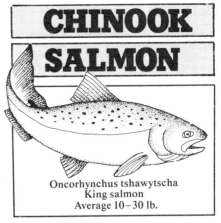

Oncorhynchus tshawytscha
King salmon
Average 10–30 lb.

How It's Caught:
Sport fishermen cast from shore and boats, using cut fish and artificial lures. Most commercial fishermen string nets in the sea or along the shoreline as salmon migrate to fresh water.

Availability:
Sliced, steaks, fillets; fresh, frozen and canned.

Nutritive Value:
High in protein and vitamin A.

Best Ways To Serve It:
Fried, sautéed or baked.

About The Sockeye Salmon:
The sockeye is sometimes called "red salmon" because of the deep red color of its flesh. It is considered one of the most valuable and abundant of all Alaska salmon. The sockeye lives in salt water for approximately four years until it matures and migrates to its spawning grounds in freshwater streams and lakes. The sockeye salmon always returns to the stream in which it was born. It dies within a few days of spawning, and its offspring return to the sea, within one year of hatching.

Where It's Caught:
In streams and lakes along the Alaska coast as far north as the Seward Peninsula. Salmon are rarely caught in open sea.

When It's Caught:
Depending on spawning runs. Usually between July and November.

How It's Caught:
Sport fishermen cast from shore and boats, using

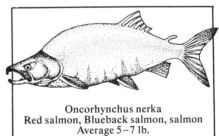

Oncorhynchus nerka
Red salmon, Blueback salmon, salmon
Average 5–7 lb.

cut fish and artificial lures. Most commercial fishermen string nets in the sea or along the shoreline

Availability:
Whole, steaks, fillets; fresh, frozen and canned.

Nutritive Value:
High in protein, vitamin A and niacin.

Best Ways To Serve It:
Fried, sautéed or baked.

89

CRABS

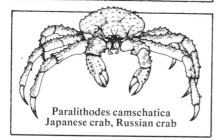

ALASKA KING CRAB

Paralithodes camschatica
Japanese crab, Russian crab

About The Alaska King Crab: The Alaska king crab
occasionally reaches weights of up to 24 pounds and measures six feet from the tip of one leg to the tip of a leg on its other side, although it usually measures half that size. It is distinguished by its heavy spine-covered shell. Like all crabs, the Alaska king crab is capable of regenerating legs torn from its body.

Where It's Caught: The Alaska king crab is found in cold waters near the poles and in water up to 1,000 feet deep. Young crabs — under three years old — live in shallow waters close to shore in schools known as "pods." Adult crabs move inshore in winter and early spring and offshore in summer

When It's Caught: December through May, when the crab is in water 60 to 200 feet deep.

How It's Caught: Nearly all Alaska king crabs are caught in crab pots baited with fish or clams.

Availability: In the shell, chunks; fresh, frozen and canned.

Nutritive Value: High in protein, thiamine and riboflavin.

Best Ways To Serve It: Baked; in salads, soups, chowders and casseroles.

BLUE CRAB

Callinectes sapidus
Average 6–8 oz.
Blue claw crab

About The Blue Crab: Male
blue crabs are called jimmies, females are called sooks, and egg-bearing females are called sponge crabs. Blue crabs about to shed their shells are called shedders or peelers; immediately after shedding and before the new shells harden they are called soft crabs. Crabs lose one or more legs during their lifetimes, but grow new ones through regen-eration. A fully grown blue crab measures five to seven inches across the back of its shell.

Where It's Caught: The blue crab inhabits the Atlantic and Gulf coasts from Massachusetts to Texas. It prefers shallow waters, and lives in bays and channels near the mouths of coastal rivers.

When It's Caught: Late July through October. Also mid-March, mid-April and mid-November.

How It's Caught: Lines and traps from shore and boats. Baits include whole and cut fish.

Availability: Live in shell; fresh or frozen cooked meat, sections, claws; frozen breaded; canned.

Nutritive Value: High in protein and vitamins, especially thiamine, niacin and riboflavin.

Best Ways To Serve It: Solid lumps of white meat from the body are used in salads. Claw meat, which is darker in color, is used in recipes where appearance is less important.

About The Dungeness Crab:
The dungeness crab, which may grow to be nine inches across its back, is one of the largest edible crabs in the United States. Its hard shell is usually a light reddish-brown or pink with a series of lighter patches; it turns bright red after it is cooked.

Where It's Caught: Along the Pacific coast from Alaska to southern California.

When It's Caught: April through September.

How It's Caught: Lines and traps from boats and shore. Baits include cut fish and scrap meat.

Availability: Live in shell; fresh or frozen cooked meat, sections, claws; frozen breaded; canned.

Nutritive Value: High in protein, thiamine, niacin and riboflavin.

Best Ways To Serve It:
Solid lumps of white meat from the body are used in salads. Claw meat,

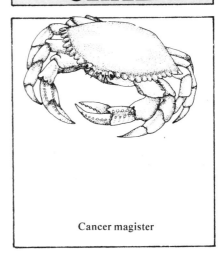

Cancer magister

which is darker in color, is used in recipes where appearance is less important.

About The Jonah Crab: The jonah crab is not of major commercial importance because it is found in areas heavily populated by lobster, and local fishermen prefer to concentrate on catching the more profitable lobster. The jonah crab's shell is red or purple and measures about six inches across its back. Because it is a walking, not swimming, crab, its claws are its most developed feature.

Where It's Caught: The jonah crab is abundant along the Atlantic coast from Maine to North Carolina. It is found near rocks in shallow water and in depths of up to 2,600 feet. It prefers clear, open water.

When It's Caught: During the spring and summer months.

Availability: Whole or sections; fresh, frozen and in jars.

Nutritive Value: High in protein, thiamine and niacin.

Best Ways To Serve It:
Baked, broiled or fried; in salads, soups, stews and chowders.

Cancer Borealis

91

RED CRAB

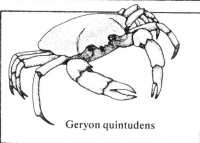

Geryon quintudens

About The Red Crab: The red crab takes its name from the bright red color of its shell before it is cooked. Scientific references to the red crab date back to 1879, but because it lives in unusually deep water, an effective trap for it was developed only recently.

Where It's Caught: The red crab lives on the continental shelf in water temperatures of 38° F. to 41° F. It lives at depths of 1,200 to 6,000 feet.

When It's Caught: Year round.

How It's Caught: Originally caught accidentally by lobster fishermen, red crabs are now caught in traps placed over mud bottoms in deep water, or with a baited trot line that may extend one mile down into the water.

Availability: Whole, sections; fresh and frozen.

Nutritive Value: High in protein, thiamine and niacin.

Best Ways To Serve It: Baked or broiled; in salads, soups, chowders and casseroles.

SOFTSHELL CRAB

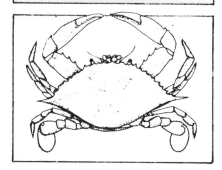

About The Softshell Crab: The term "softshell crab" refers not to a species but to a crab that has shed its hard, protective shell and has not yet grown a new one. In this stage, the crab is covered only by a thin, elastic shell which allows its body to grow. When the hard shell falls off, the crab immediately expands by about one third its original size. Before the soft, elastic shell hardens, the crab is especially vulnerable to predators, including hardshell crabs. Softshell crabs, especially of the blue crab species, are considered a delicacy.

Where It's Caught: Softshell crabs seek out secluded places within their natural range. Check the native habitats of specific species.

When It's Caught: Shedding takes place only during warm months, so softshell crabs can be found in late spring, summer and early fall.

How It's Caught: A professional crab fisherman can determine how soon a crab will shed and sorts the crabs accordingly. A white-colored crab, called a "green crab", will not shed for more than a week and will probably be sent to market as a hardshell crab. A pink or red crab will shed in less than a week; this crab will be held until it sheds and will then be shipped to market as a softshell crab.

Availability: Whole, fresh and frozen.

Nutritive Value: High in protein.

Best Ways To Serve It: Pan-fried.

About The Tanner Crab: A member of the spider crab family, the tanner crab has long, slender legs and a rounded body. Like the Alaska king crab, the tanner crab has a hard, spine – covered shell. It grows up to two and one – half pounds.

Where It's Caught: The tanner crab is found in the eastern Pacific from the Bering Straits and the Aleutian Islands to the Cortex Bank, opposite the boundary dividing Mexico and the United States. In the Atlantic, it is found from the west coast of Greenland to the Maine coast.

When It's Caught: Throughout the winter and spring.

How It's Caught: Nearly all tanner crabs are caught in crab pots baited with fish or clams.

Availability: Whole crabs, sec-

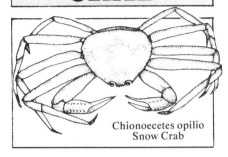

Chionoecetes opilio
Snow Crab

tions; frozen.

Nutritive Value: High in protein, thiamine and riboflavin.

Best Ways To Serve It:
Baked or broiled; in salads, soups, chowders and casseroles.

LOBSTER

About The American Lobster: In the 18th and 19th centuries, lobster was so abundant that it was used as bait to catch the more highly esteemed cod and striped bass. Today, lobster are so sought after and expensive that some restaurants have dropped them from their menus. The American lobster is the most valuable commercial lobster available in the United States. It occasionally reaches weights up to 45 pounds, and even at this large size the meat remains tender.

The lobster has two claws — a small, thin claw for seizing prey and a large, heavy claw for crushing the prey.

Where It's Caught: The American lobster is plentiful in the waters of Nova Scotia, Newfoundland and Maine, in depths of 10 to 200 feet. Lobster fishermen who drag the bottom of water more than 600 feet deep occasionally catch extremely large lobsters.

When It's Caught: Year round, but most are caught in the spring and summer months.

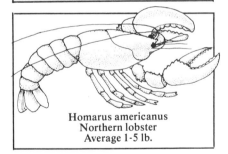

Homarus americanus
Northern lobster
Average 1-5 lb.

How It's Caught: In traps called lobster pots, oblong boxes made of widely spaced wood planks to allow small lobsters to escape.

Availability: Lobster are sold live, whole cooked in the shell, frozen raw and boiled, and as frozen, fresh and canned

Nutritive Value: High in protein, thiamine and niacin.

Best Ways To Serve It:
Boiled, steamed, broiled or barbecued.

SPINY LOBSTER

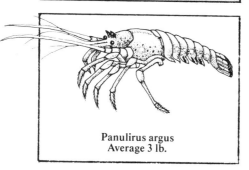

Panulirus argus
Average 3 lb.

About The Spiny Lobster:
Although related to the lobster, the spiny lobster is actually a sea-dwelling crayfish. It does not have the large, heavy claw of a true lobster and its body and legs are covered with thin spines. The spiny lobster is an unusually beautiful shellfish, marked with shades of brown, yellow, green, orange and blue. It occasionally reaches weights up to 17 pounds.

Where It's Caught: In the western Atlantic from North Carolina to Brazil, in the southern Gulf of Mexico and in the Caribbean Sea. A close relative of the spiny lobster is caught off the coast of California.

When It's Caught: Year round.

How It's Caught: In baited lobster pots along the ocean's bottom.

Availability: Live, whole, boiled; fresh and frozen. Spiny lobster is often marketed as "rock lobster" and is the source of most lobster tails served in restaurants.

Nutritive Value: High in protein, thiamine and niacin.

Best Ways To Serve It: Boiled or broiled; in salads and chowders.

SHRIMP

BROWN SHRIMP

Penaeus axtecus

About The Brown Shrimp:
A crustacean, the shrimp got its name from the Swedish word "skrympa," which means shrink. The shrimp has 10 legs and casts off its hard outer shell to allow its body to grow. A new shell grows to replace the old one. Shrimp usually swim forward, but can also propel themselves backwards at great speeds. The brown shrimp is reddish brown when raw.

Where It's Caught: In the Gulf of Mexico off Texas, Alabama, Florida and Mexico.

When It's Caught: Year round, usually at night.

How It's Caught: In nets, baited pots and otter trawls.

Availability: Shrimp are sold according to size and are most often referred to as jumbo, large, medium and small. They are available raw or cooked, peeled or unpeeled, fresh or frozen.

Nutritive Value: High in protein, thiamine and niacin.

Best Ways To Serve It: Steamed, boiled, fried or sautéed.

About The Rock Shrimp:

Rock shrimp look very much like miniature lobster tails. The rock shrimp takes its name from its extremely tough exoskeleton. It has been included in the commercial shrimp industry only since the 1970's; before that it was discarded because its hard shell made it too difficult to peel. New machinery has been developed to peel the rock shrimp, and now several million pounds are harvested each year.

Where It's Caught: In the Atlantic Ocean off the Virginia coast, and in the Gulf of Mexico.

When It's Caught: Year round, although local authorities may limit the season as a conservation measure.

How It's Caught: In nets and otter trawls.

Availability: Peeled; fresh and frozen.

Nutritive Value: High in protein, thiamine and niacin.

Best Ways To Serve It: Broiled, boiled, pan-fried or sautéed.

ROCK SHRIMP

Sicyonia brevirostris

About The White Shrimp:

The shrimp is considered the most valuable of all seafood. The white shrimp, which is greenish gray in color, is one of the most commercially important shrimp.

Where It's Caught: In shallow waters of bays, primarily in Louisiana.

When It's Caught: Year round.

How It's Caught: In nets, baited pots and otter trawls.

Availability: Shrimp are sold according to size and are most often referred to as jumbo, large, medium and small. They are available raw or cooked, peeled or unpeeled, fresh and frozen.

Nutritive Value: High in protein, thiamine and niacin.

Best Ways To Serve It: Steamed, boiled, fried or sautéed.

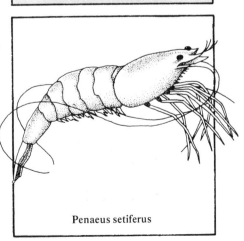

WHITE SHRIMP

Penaeus setiferus

CRAYFISH

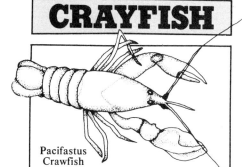

CRAYFISH

Pacifastus
Crawfish

About The Crayfish: A crustacean, the crayfish resembles the lobster. It ranges in size from one inch to eight pounds, although it is considered edible only if it is longer than 3½ inches. Crayfish are regarded as a delicacy throughout the southern United States and in many other countries. In Finland and Sweden, summer festivals called krebfests are dedicated to the consumption of crayfish.

Where It's Caught: Crayfish are found in freshwater lakes and streams on every continent except Africa. They are abundant in slow-moving streams along the Pacific coastline and in streams from Wisconsin through Maine and in the Alleghany Mountains. Most Louisiana crayfish are caught in the southern portion of the state.

When It's Caught: Year round.
How It's Caught: Crayfish can be caught individually under rocks in a shallow stream bed by grabbing them by hand or with a net. Crayfish to be marketed are harvested with nets and baited traps.

Availability: Crayfish are not usually available in most areas of the country. In Louisiana, where most crafish are consumed, about two-thirds of all crayfish sold are marketed live.

Nutritive Value: High in protein and phosphorus.

Best Ways To Serve It:
Boiled; in soups and chowders.

BIVALVES

CLAMS

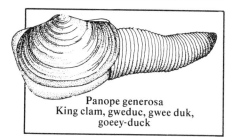

GEODUCK CLAM

Panope generosa
King clam, gweduc, gwee duk,
goeey-duck

About The Geoduck Clam:
The geoduck is the largest American clam. Its neck, or siphon, is so large that it cannot be drawn into its nearly rectangular shell. The shell always remains open slightly to reveal the brown mantle that hides the body of the clam inside.

Where It's Caught: All along the West coast of the United States, but it is most abundant in Washington's Puget Sound. The geoduck lives in mud, sand, small gravel or a mixture of these, from 18 inches to six feet below the beach surface or, if underwater, beneath the bottom surface.

When It's Caught: Year round.
How It's Caught: Commercially harvested geoduck are caught by divers at depths of 10 to 60 feet.

Availability: Steaks, chunks; fresh, frozen and canned.
Nutritive Value: High in protein.
Best Ways To Serve It:
Fried; in chowders.

About The Littleneck Clam:

There are two kinds of littleneck clams—a species known as littleneck (one word) and the marketing term "Little Neck" (two words), which refers to three and four year old quahogs, the smallest quahogs commercially available. The Little Neck (small quahog) is named for the Little Neck Bay on Long Island, once the center of the half-shell clam industry. The littleneck species (protothaca staminea) is not a quahog and should not be eaten raw.

Where It's Caught: Along the Pacific coastline from Alaska to California.

When It's Caught: Year round, although local authorities may limit the season as a conservation measure.

How It's Caught: Small numbers of littleneck clams can be gathered by hand or with tongs; com-

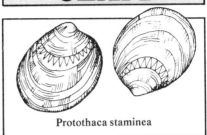

LITTLENECK CLAM

Protothaca staminea

mercial clamming vessels use dredges.

Availability: Live, in the shell, shucked; fresh and frozen.

Nutritive Value: High in protein.

Best Ways To Serve It: Baked, steamed, broiled or fried; in salads, dips and chowders.

About The Razor Clam:

The razor clam has a long, narrow shell that resembles a straight-edged razor. It is not as commercially important as many other clams because it lives in an area where the more highly esteemed quahog is abundant, and clammers tend to harvest the quahog instead of the razor. Because its meat is very chewy, the razor clam is rarely eaten on the half shell.

Where It's Caught: Razor clams are found along the coast of California from the tideline to depths of up to 90 feet.

When It's Caught: Year round, but local authorities may limit the season as a conservation measure.

How It's Caught: Unlike most other clams, the razor clam shouldn't be located by treading barefoot over a clam bed because the edges of its shell are extremely sharp. It can't be raked because the shell is fragile and easily broken. The clam is located by the small hole it makes in moist sand with its siphon as it breathes; it is gathered by digging quickly with a

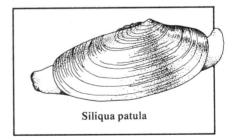

RAZOR CLAM

Siliqua patula

narrow bladed shovel about four inches from the hole. When the clam realizes it is being pursued it burrows more deeply in the sand. Some commercial clammers use powerful water jets that force the razor clam from its bed.

Availability: Live in the shell, shucked; fresh and frozen.

Nutritive Value: High in protein.

Best Ways To Serve It: Steamed or fried.

SOFT
SHELL
CLAM

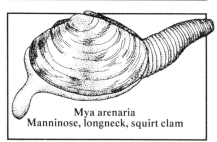

Mya arenaria
Manninose, longneck, squirt clam

About The Soft Shell Clam:
The soft shell clam can be identified by its long neck, or siphon, which protrudes from its shell. Its hiding place can be located easily because it spurts a stream of water into the air from its siphon when it senses footsteps nearby.

Where It's Caught: The soft shell clam burrows in the mud along the coastline. It is most abundant in the Chesapeake Bay, where salinity levels are low.

When It's Caught: Year round, although local authorities may limit the season as a conservation measure.

How It's Caught: The soft shell clam can be located by treading barefoot over muddy bottoms and gathered by hand or with rakes and tongs; commercial vessels use hydraulic dredges.

Availability: Whole, minced; fresh, frozen and canned.

Nutritive Value: High in protein.

Best Ways To Serve It:
Steamed or fried; in chowders.

SURF
CLAM

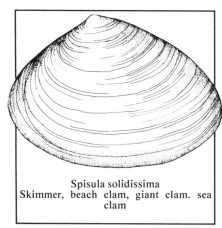

Spisula solidissima
Skimmer, beach clam, giant clam. sea clam

About The Surf Clam:
The surf clam's shell was once used as wampum and decoration by American Indian tribes. The shell is nearly triangular with a shiny, light brown surface. Its meat is tough and sandy, but it can be cleaned and tenderized. The surf clam is the most commercially important clam caught along the Atlantic shore, and it accounts for nearly all canned clams.

Where It's Caught: The surf clam is found in depths of up to 90 feet, just below the bottom surface. It is abundant along the Atlantic coast from New England to Maryland.

When It's Caught: Year round, although local authorities may limit its season as a conservation measure.

How It's Caught: Small numbers of surf clams can be gathered by hand or with rakes and tongs; commercial vessels use dredges.

Availability: Live in the shell, shucked; fresh, frozen and canned.

Nutritive Value: High in protein.

Best Ways To Serve It:
Baked, steamed, broiled or fried; in salads, dips and chowders.

About The Quahog: One of the most abundant and commercially important clams, the quahog is marketed under a variety of names. A small quahog, three or four years old, is called a Little Neck Clam (named for the Little Neck Bay on Long Island); a slightly larger quahog is called a cherrystone (named for the Cherrystone Creek in Virginia); and any quahog larger than a cherrystone is called a chowder clam.

Where It's Caught: In the Atlantic Ocean along the New England coast. The quahog is found in depths of 36 to 540 feet, although most are caught at 90 to 150 feet.

When It's Caught: Year round, although local authorities may limit the season as a conservation measure.

How It's Caught: Quahogs can be gathered with rakes or tongs; commercial vessels use hydraulic dredges.

Availability: Live in the shell,

QUAHOG

Arctica islandica
Hard clam, mahogany clam,
Little Neck, cherrystone

shucked; fresh and frozen.

Nutritive Value: High in protein.

Best Ways To Serve It: On the half shell, steamed or fried.

MUSSELS

About The Blue Mussel: Like all mussels, the blue mussel is a bivalve mollusk. It is the most common of all sea mussels and is found in large groups growing on gravel, rocks, jetties and any other surface that will support it. The mussel attaches itself to a surface by a thin silky thread that it secretes. The blue mussel is distinguished by its smooth, dark blue shell. The shell's interior is gleaming white.

Where It's Caught: Along the Atlantic coast from Nova Scotia to North Carolina. It is especially abundant off the coast of New England.

When It's Caught: Year round, although blue mussels are best from September through April.

How It's Caught: Mussels are gathered by hand off the surfaces on which they grow. Wooden frames and stakes are sometimes placed in the

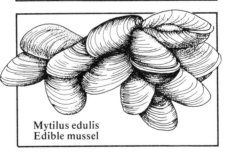

BLUE
MUSSEL

Mytilus edulis
Edible mussel

water to encourage mussels to settle.

Availability: Live, in tightly closed shells.

Nutritive Value: High in protein and vitamin A.

Best Ways To Serve It: Steamed, whole or on the half shell.

OYSTERS

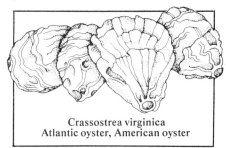

EASTERN OYSTER

Crassostrea virginica
Atlantic oyster, American oyster

About The Eastern Oyster:

The term "oyster" refers to more than 100 species of bivalve mollusks, and of all these the eastern oyster is the most commercially important. It accounts for approximately 85 percent of all the oysters sold in the United States. All oysters live inside two unmatched shells— the upper shell is flat, the lower shell concave—joined by a ligament. The shells are watertight, and an adductor muscle allows the oyster to open and close its shell. Normally sedentary, a young oyster "glues" itself to a support surface with a secretion from its body and never moves again.

Where It's Caught: All oysters live in shallow, brackish waters along the coasts of temperate or tropical waters. The eastern oyster is found along the North Atlantic coast from the Gulf of St. Lawrence to the Gulf of Mexico.

When It's Caught: Oysters are edible all year round, but are best during the fall and winter months.

How It's Caught: Gathered by hand; with long-handled tongs from boats. Most commercially gathered oysters are harvested with a power dredge.

Availability: Live in the shell, shucked; fresh, frozen and canned.

Nutritive Value: High in niacin and thiamine.

Best Ways To Serve It:
Raw, steamed or fried.

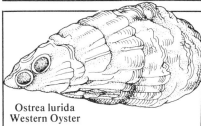

OLYMPIA OYSTER

Ostrea lurida
Western Oyster

About The Olympia Oyster:

A bivalve mollusk, the oyster has been cultivated and eaten for centuries. The earliest recorded documentation of oyster cultivation dates back to 1620 in Japan, but it is believed that oysters were gathered long before that time. In North America, the olympia oyster is regarded as a delicacy. Because large quantities were harvested to meet this demand, it is not as abundant as it once was and accounts for only a small percentage of the commercial harvest.

Where It's Caught: The olympia oyster is native to the Pacific.

When It's Caught: It should be harvested in the fall and winter.

How It's Caught: Oysters can be gathered from their beds by hand, harvested from boats with long-handled tongs, or, most economically, power dredged.

Availability: Live in the shell, shucked; fresh, frozen and canned.

Nutritive Value: High in niacin and thiamine.

Best Ways To Serve It:
Raw, steamed or fried.

About The Pacific Oyster:

Currently the most important of West Coast oysters, the Pacific oyster was originally imported from Japan. It was introduced to North American waters after experimental plantings of the eastern oyster failed to thrive in the Pacific. The Pacific oyster accounts for nearly 15 percent of the commercially available oysters in the United States.

Where It's Caught: In shallow coastal waters from Alaska to northern California.

When It's Caught: Oysters are available year round, but they are most flavorful in the fall and winter months. They spawn in the summer months, and their flesh tends to be thin and watery then.

How It's Caught: Gathered by

PACIFIC OYSTER

Crassostrea gigas
Pacific king oyster

hand, tongs, or power dredge.

Availability: Live in the shell, shucked; fresh, frozen and canned.

Nutritive Value: High in niacin.

Best Ways To Serve It: Raw, steamed or fried.

SCALLOPS

About The Bay Scallop:

The flute-edged shell of the bay scallop has long been admired for its beauty. Like clams and oysters, the scallop is a two-shelled mollusk, but it is far more active than other shellfish. It swims by opening and closing its shells to propel itself through the water. This motion develops its adductor muscle, the only part of the scallop eaten by Americans. Europeans eat all the meat of the scallop. The bay scallop is smaller and less plentiful than the sea scallop and is considered more valuable.

Where It's Caught: Bay scallops are found in bays from New England southward to the Gulf of Mexico.

When It's Caught: Although scallops are available year round, most areas restrict their harvesting to April through October as a conservation measure.

How It's Caught: In shallow waters, bay scallops are harvested with dip nets, rakes or by hand. In

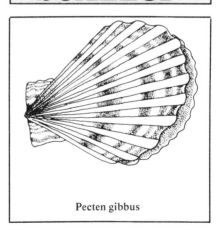

BAY SCALLOP

Pecten gibbus

deeper water, they are gathered with dredges.

Availability: Fresh and frozen.

Nutritive Value: High in protein and niacin.

Best Ways To Serve It: Pan-fried, sautéed or broiled.

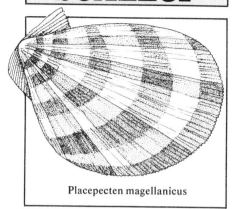

SEA SCALLOP

Placepecten magellanicus

About The Sea Scallop: The sea scallop is the most commercially important scallop in the United States, accounting for the majority of scallops sold. Its saucer-shaped shell was once used by American Indian tribes as ornaments, and today it is sought by collectors for use as decorations. Larger shells are used as serving dishes for some types of seafood. The shell of the sea scallop is not as delicate as the shell of the bay scallop.

Where It's Caught: Most commercially harvested sea scallops are found in the deep waters on the Atlantic, off the northern and middle Atlantic states. The former whaling port of New Bedford, Massachussetts, is the greatest source of sea scallops.

When It's Caught: To prevent the supply of sea scallops from being depleted, most states restrict fishing to April through November.

How It's Caught: Sea scallops are harvested with dredges.

Availability: Fresh and frozen.

Nutritive Value: High in protein and niacin.

Best Ways To Serve It: Pan-fried, sautéed or broiled.

UNIVALVES

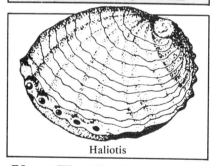

ABALONE

Haliotis

About The Abalone: The abalone is a mollusk whose generic name, "haliotis," is derived from two Greek words meaning "sea ear" because of its resemblance to a human ear. The abalone's inner shell, with its shimmering colors, is prized for use in jewelry and other decorations. This shell protects the abalone while permitting its muscular foot to maneuver along the ocean floor or cling by suction to a surface.

Where It's Caught: Along the Pacific coast from Alaska to Mexico. Commercial harvesting is strictly regulated in California.

When It's Caught: Year round.

How It's Caught: Small numbers of abalone can be gathered by hand in shallow waters; divers use knives to pry abalone loose from the surfaces they rest on. Baited traps are usually used to harvest large numbers of abalone.

Availability: The abalone is marketed fresh in California. Frozen abalone meat is occasionally available elsewhere.

Nutritive Value: High in protein.

Best Ways To Serve It: Raw or sautéed; in chowders.

CEPHALOPODS

About The Octopus: The octopus is best-known in North America for its appearances in horror movies, although its meat is considered a delicacy in China, Japan, Spain, Portugal, Italy and Greece. Like the squid, the octopus is a mollusk. It has a flexible, nearly round body with eight long tentacles equipped with suction cups. These cups are used to catch lobsters, crabs, clams and scallops, which comprise most of the octopus' diet. The average octopus found at market weighs about three pounds.

Where It's Caught: Nearly all commercially harvested octopus are found off the Pacific coast from Alaska to Baja California. The octopus are usually found about one mile offshore in depths of 100 to 200 feet.

When It's Caught: Year round.

How It's Caught: In cone-shaped baskets known as "devilfish pots."

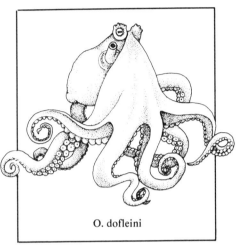

OCTOPUS

O. dofleini

Availability: Gutted; fresh and frozen.

Nutritive Value: High in thiamine and niacin.

Best Ways To Serve It: Raw, as sashimi, or stewed.

About The Squid: It appears that some of the stories about monsters inhabiting the sea may have been inspired by squid sightings. Giant squid with tentacles 40 feet long have been observed at depths of 1,500 feet. Most squid, however, are considerably smaller — 10 to 12 inches long — and are used as food or bait. The squid is a mollusk, and is sometimes referred to as an inside-out shellfish because of its thin internal shell. The squid uses its tentacles to grasp its prey.

Where It's Caught: The squid is found in waters off southern California and New England and the middle Atlantic. It prefers deep waters, but moves closer to shore to spawn.

When It's Caught: January, February, April, May and June.

How It's Caught: Lampara nets.

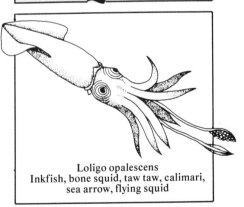

SQUID

Loligo opalescens
Inkfish, bone squid, taw taw, calimari, sea arrow, flying squid

Availability: Whole; fresh and frozen.

Nutritive Value: High in protein and phosphorus.

Best Ways To Serve It: Pan-fried, deep-fried or boiled.

COOKING THE CATCH

When you sit down to eat a meal, you're doing more than simply providing your body with the nutrients it needs to function efficiently. You're also giving yourself time to relax and enjoy the flavor and texture of different foods. Your diet should be varied and enjoyable, including foods and combinations of dishes that offer variety and excitement. Seafood can be delicious and satisfying, and can be prepared in hundreds of innovative ways. Remember, a recipe is a guide that suggests the proper balances of ingredients and seasonings. Although it is designed to be followed directly, you can also vary it to suit your own tastes.

Cooking The Catch gives you a chance to sample the species profiled in *The Fish And The Shellfish.* These recipes, which range from the extremely simple to the moderately complex, are divided into five categories: Sauces; Hors d'oeuvres, Snacks & Salads; Soups, Stews and Casseroles; Entrées; and Low Calorie dishes.

Near the top of each recipe, you'll see a silhouette of a fish with a small number inside. These numbers correspond to the edibility profiles detailed in *The Fish And The Shellfish.* The number refers to the edibility profile of the fish featured in the recipe. If that particular fish isn't available, or if you'd prefer to substitute something else, simply refer back to *The Fish And The Shellfish.* To match the recipe select any fish from the same edibility profile category as the one shown on the recipe. Because fish within the same category have similar flavor qualities, the recipe will turn out properly even with a substitution. A fish from another category will result in an enjoyable dish with a different flavor.

If you have a specific type of fish you'd like to prepare, check the chapter index. You can use any recipe listed for that specific fish, or any recipe that uses a fish with the same edibility profile number.

In each of the recipes, the ingredients are listed in the order in which they'll be used. Estimated preparation and cooking times are included at the bottom of the list of ingredients to give you a general idea of how much time you'll need to prepare each dish. If a dish doesn't have a distinct cooking time but is simply simmered or sautéed as other ingredients are added, it has been assigned only a preparation, not a cooking, time.

For your convenience, the instruction portion of each recipe is divided into short paragraphs. Each new paragraph signals the beginning of a new step or procedure, and is indicated by a small black fish near the left-hand margin.

Many of the recipes are representative of different regions of the country, while others have historical significance. Others were chosen just for their simplicity or culinary appeal. Several of the appetizers and sauces require no cooking, just a blending of ingredients. Each of the low calorie recipes is accompanied by its calorie count.

While the recipes are clear and the instructions easy to follow, it is always advisable to read through a recipe once before you begin cooking.

AMANDINE SAUCE

| ½ cup margarine or butter | 1 tablespoon lemon juice |
| 1 cup blanched sliced almonds | |

PREPARATION TIME: 5 MINUTES

In heavy fry pan melt margarine over low heat.

Add almonds and continue heating, stirring until margarine and almonds turn light brown. Add lemon juice. Makes ½ cup sauce.

 # BÉARNAISE SAUCE

1 tablespoon chopped green onion	¼ teaspoon dried chervil leaves
2 teaspoons lemon juice	3 egg yolks
¼ cup dry white wine	⅛ teaspoon cayenne pepper
½ teaspoon dried tarragon leaves	½ cup margarine or butter

PREPARATION TIME: 15 MINUTES

In a small saucepan combine green onion, lemon juice, white wine, tarragon and chervil. Simmer until mixture is reduced to about 2 tablespoons. Cool.

Place egg yolks, cayenne and herb mixture in blender; cover. Turn blender on and off quickly.

Heat margarine until melted and almost boiling. Turn blender on high speed and, lifting cover slightly, pour in margarine slowly, blending until thick and fluffy (about 30 seconds).

Heat in double boiler over warm (not hot) water until ready to serve. Makes 1 cup sauce.

 # BORDELAISE SAUCE

½ cup chopped fresh mushrooms	2 teaspoons dried, crushed tarragon
1 tablespoon margarine or butter	2 tablespoons lemon juice
3 tablespoons cornstarch	3 tablespoons red wine
2 cups fish stock or chicken broth	¼ teaspoon white pepper

PREPARATION TIME: 10 MINUTES   COOKING TIME: 5–10 MINUTES

Cook mushrooms in margarine or butter until tender.

continued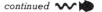

In a large bowl mix cornstarch and stock; stir into mushrooms gradually. Cook, stirring constantly, until boiling.

Add remaining ingredients and simmer 5 to 10 minutes. Makes 2¼ cups sauce.

BUTTER SAUCE

2 tablespoons finely chopped green onion	⅛ teaspoon ground black pepper
½ cup dry white wine	½ lb. butter at
1 teaspoon white wine vinegar	room temperature

PREPARATION TIME: 15 MINUTES

In a heavy saucepan combine onion, wine, vinegar, and pepper.

Cook over high flame, stirring vigorously with a wire whisk. Add butter, about a tablespoon at a time, while continuing to beat. Never allow sauce to boil.

When all the butter has been added, continue beating rapidly while removing saucepan from heat. Place on a cool surface. (Mixture should not be chilled, but if it is excessively hot the ingredients will separate.)

Until the sauce is served, continue to stir at intervals. Makes 1½ cups sauce.

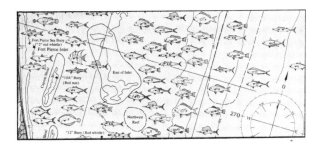

DILL SAUCE

Recommended for seafood cocktails and salads.

¾ cup mayonnaise	½ teaspoon sugar
½ cup sour cream	½ teaspoon salt
¾ teaspoon dill weed	Dash of pepper

PREPARATION TIME: 10 MINUTES

Combine all ingredients thoroughly and chill.

Makes approximately 1¼ cups sauce.

SAUCES

 # HOLLANDAISE SAUCE

| 3 egg yolks | Dash of cayenne pepper |
| 2 tablespoons lemon juice | ½ cup margarine or butter |

PREPARATION TIME: 15 MINUTES

 Place egg yolks, lemon juice and cayenne pepper in blender; cover. Turn blender on and off quickly.

 Heat margarine or butter until melted and nearly boiling. Turn blender on high speed and, lifting cover slightly, pour in margarine slowly, blending until the mixture is thick and fluffy (about 30 seconds).

 Heat in a double boiler over warm (not hot) water until ready to serve. Makes 1 cup sauce.

 # HORSERADISH SAUCE

½ cup horseradish	½ teaspoon salt
1 tablespoon flour	1 cup half-and-half
¼ teaspoon paprika	

PREPARATION TIME: 5 MINUTES   COOKING TIME: 5 MINUTES

 In a small saucepan combine horseradish, flour, paprika and salt. Stir in half-and-half.

 Cook until thickened, stirring constantly. Makes approximately 1½ cups sauce.

 # LEMON CREAM SAUCE

1½ cups sour cream	1 teaspoon grated lemon rind
3 oz. cream cheese (1 pkg.)	1 teaspoon horseradish
1 tablespoon lemon juice	¼ teaspoon salt
1 tablespoon chopped parsley	

PREPARATION TIME: 10 MINUTES

 Combine all ingredients and chill. Makes 1 cup sauce.

MORNAY SAUCE

Especially recommended with baked or broiled fillets.

¼ cup margarine or butter	2 cups milk
3 tablespoons flour	¼ cup grated Parmesan cheese
1 teaspoon salt	2 egg yolks, beaten
⅛ teaspoon white pepper	

PREPARATION TIME: 15 MINUTES

 Melt margarine or butter in a small saucepan.

 Stir in flour, salt, and pepper. Add milk gradually and cook over low heat, stirring constantly, until thick and smooth. Stir in Parmesan cheese.

 Stir a little of the hot mixture into the yolks and add yolks to remaining mixture, stirring constantly. Makes approximately 2½ cups sauce.

TARTAR SAUCE

1 cup mayonnaise	2 tablespoons chopped
¼ cup sour cream	Spanish olives
2 tablespoons chopped dill pickle	1 teaspoon lemon juice
2 tablespoons finely chopped onion	Dash of pepper

PREPARATION TIME: 10 MINUTES

 Combine all ingredients and chill. Makes 2 cups of sauce.

HORS D'OEUVRES, SNACKS & SALADS

 # ALASKAN APPETIZER PIE

1 can (6½ oz.) king crab meat or other crab meat	1 cup chili sauce
1 pkg. (8 oz.) cream cheese, softened	½ cup chopped parsley
	Melba toast

PREPARATION TIME: 10 MINUTES (plus chilling time).

 Drain crab meat; flake. Remove any remaining pieces of shell or cartilage.

continued 〰️ ▶

Spread cream cheese in bottom of a 9-inch glass pie plate. Cover with chili sauce. Top with flaked crab meat. Sprinkle parsley on top of crab meat.

▶ Chill. Serve with melba toast. Makes three cups of spread.

 # CAVIAR CROWN

1 jar (4 oz.) salmon caviar	2 tablespoons chopped
1 jar (3½ oz.) whitefish caviar	green onion
2 pkg. (8 oz. each) cream	1 teaspoon Worcestershire sauce
cheese, softened	Parsley
2 tablespoons lemon juice	Assorted crackers or melba toast

PREPARATION TIME: 15 MINUTES

▶ Drain caviars.
▶ Combine cheese and seasonings.
▶ Place cheese mixture in the center of a serving plate and shape it into a circle about 7 inches in diameter and 1 inch thick.
▶ Cover a 4-inch circle in the center with salmon caviar. Cover the area around that circle on top of the cheese mixture with whitefish caviar. Place small sprigs of parsley around the edge of the salmon caviar.*
▶ Garnish base of cheese mixture with parsley.
▶ Serve with crackers or melba toast. Makes approximately two cups of spread.

*You may substitute a ring of overlapping slices of small stuffed olives or a ribbon of cream cheese from a pastry tube for the parsley if you prefer.

 # CLAMDIGGER DIP

1 can (7½ or 8 oz.)	1 teaspoon chopped parsley
minced clams	¼ teaspoon salt
1 teaspoon Worcestershire sauce	⅛ teaspoon liquid hot pepper
1 pkg. (8 oz.) cream cheese,	sauce
softened	Assorted chips, crackers and/or
1 tablespoon lemon juice	raw vegetables
1 tablespoon grated onion	

PREPARATION TIME: 10 MINUTES (plus chilling time).

▶ Drain clams and reserve liquid.
▶ Add seasonings and clams to thoroughly softened cream cheese. Mix well. Chill at least 1 hour to allow flavors to blend. If the dip is too thick, gradually add clam liquid.
▶ Serve with chips, crackers or vegetables. Makes approximately 1⅓ cups of dip.

CRISPY SCALLOP SALAD

1½ lb. scallops, fresh or frozen	1½ cups diagonally sliced
1½ cups water	celery
3 tablespoons lemon juice	6 servings crisp salad greens
½ teaspoon salt	¾ cup sliced radishes
3 peppercorns	3 hard-cooked eggs, sliced
3 slices onion	1 pint cherry tomatoes, halved,
½ cup tarragon vinegar	or 2 medium tomatoes, cut
⅓ cup salad oil	into wedges
⅓ cup sugar	¼ lb. cheddar cheese, cut in
1 clove garlic, sliced	thin strips

PREPARATION TIME: 25 MINUTES

► Thaw scallops if frozen. Rinse with cold water to remove any remaining shell particles; drain well.

► Combine water, lemon juice, ½ teaspoon salt, peppercorns and onion in saucepan; bring to a boil. Add scallops. Reduce heat and simmer 3 to 5 minutes or until scallops are tender; drain.

► Combine vinegar, oil, sugar, remaining teaspoon salt and garlic; stir until sugar is dissolved. Pour over scallops. Cover and chill several hours.

► Add celery to scallops. Mix and drain; save marinade.

► Arrange greens in a large salad bowl. Pile scallops and celery in center of bowl and arrange remaining foods in groups around scallops on greens. Serve with reserved marinade or with your favorite French or oil-and-vinegar salad dressing. Serves six.

 # DOWN EAST PÂTÉ

2 cans (3¾ or 4 oz. each)	3 tablespoons lemon juice
sardines	2 tablespoons grated onion
2 pkgs. (8 oz. each) cream	2 tablespoons chopped parsley
cheese, softened	½ cup chopped parsley
1 tablespoon horseradish	Assorted breads, crackers
2 drops hot pepper sauce	and/or raw vegetables
½ cup crushed potato chips	

PREPARATION TIME: 10 MINUTES

► Drain and mash sardines.

► Add onion, horseradish, lemon juice, 2 tablespoons parsley and mashed sardines to softened cream cheese. Mix thoroughly and shape mixture into a mound on a serving plate.

► Combine potato chips and ½ cup parsley and cover the mixture completely. Chill.

► Serve with breads, crackers or vegetables. Makes approximately 3 cups.

HOT FISH SALAD

1 lb. fish fillets	1 jar (2 oz.) sliced pimientos
2 cups chopped celery	2 tablespoons chopped green
½ cup chopped green peppers	onion
½ cup slivered almonds	2 tablespoons lemon juice
½ cup mayonnaise	½ teaspoon salt
1 can (13 oz.) cream of celery	2 cups crushed potato chips
soup	½ cup grated sharp cheese

PREPARATION TIME: 10 MINUTES   COOKING TIME: 25–27 MINUTES

◗ Cut fish in ½-inch pieces.
◗ In a large mixing bowl, combine fish and all other ingredients except chips and cheese. Pour into a casserole dish.
◗ Bake at 350° F. for 20 minutes.
◗ Remove from oven and sprinkle with chips and cheese.
◗ Return to oven for 5 to 7 minutes more or until cheese melts.
◗ Sprinkle lightly with paprika. Serves six.

 # INDIVIDUAL ANTIPASTO SALAD

1 can (3½ or 3 ¾ oz.) albacore	2 ripe olives
or other solid-pack tuna	1 green onion
Crisp salad greens	½ hard-cooked egg
⅓ cup potato salad	1 teaspoon capers
3 or 4 cucumber slices	2 tablespoons mayonnaise
2 radishes	Lemon wedges for garnish
2 carrot sticks or curls	

PREPARATION TIME: 10 MINUTES

◗ Drain oil from tuna and turn tuna onto a serving plate lined with salad greens.
◗ Arrange potato salad, cucumber, radishes, carrot, olives, onion and egg around tuna.
◗ Combine capers and mayonnaise.
◗ Serve with caper and mayonnaise mixture and lemon. Makes one salad.

LOBSTER BOATS

½ lb. cooked lobster meat, fresh or frozen	2 tablespoons mayonnaise or salad dressing
24 fresh mushrooms, approximately 1½" in diameter	¼ teaspoon Worcestershire sauce
¼ cup condensed cream of mushroom soup	⅛ teaspoon liquid hot pepper sauce
2 tablespoons fine soft bread crumbs	Dash of pepper
	Grated Parmesan cheese

PREPARATION TIME: 10 MINUTES   COOKING TIME: 10–15 MINUTES

▶ Thaw lobster meat if frozen. Drain and remove any remaining shell or cartilage. Chop the meat.

▶ Rinse mushrooms in cold water; then dry and remove stems.

▶ Combine soup, crumbs, mayonnaise or salad dressing, seasonings, and lobster.

▶ Stuff each mushroom cap with a tablespoonful of the mixture. Sprinkle with cheese.

▶ Place mushrooms on a well-greased baking pan and bake at 400° F. for 10 to 15 minutes or until lightly browned. Makes 24 lobster boats.

NEW ORLEANS CRAB SPREAD

1 can (12 oz.) blue crab meat or other crab meat, fresh or frozen	3 tablespoons chopped pimiento
	2 tablespoons chopped green onion
2 cans (6½ or 7½ oz. each) crab meat	1 teaspoon salt
¼ cup tarragon vinegar	½ teaspoon freshly ground pepper
⅓ cup mayonnaise or salad dressing	1 tablespoon drained capers
	Assorted chips, crackers and/or raw vegetables

PREPARATION TIME: 40 MINUTES

▶ Thaw crab meat if frozen. Drain and remove any remaining shell or cartilage. Flake the crab meat and pour vinegar over it.

▶ Chill for 30 minutes; then drain.

▶ Add mayonnaise, pimiento, onion, salt and pepper. Mix thoroughly. Garnish with capers.

▶ Serve with chips, crackers or vegetables. Makes approximately 2 cups.

NUTTY OYSTERS*

2 cans (12 oz. each) oysters	¼ teaspoon salt
¼ cup toasted blanched slivered almonds	Dash nutmeg
	Dash pepper
2 cups fine soft bread crumbs	½ cup fine dry bread crumbs
1 egg, beaten	Fat for frying
1 tablespoon chopped onion	1 cup seafood cocktail sauce*
1 tablespoon chopped parsley	

PREPARATION TIME: 10 MINUTES   COOKING TIME: 2–3 MINUTES

▶ Drain oysters thoroughly.

▶ Chop almonds and oysters. Combine almonds, oysters, bread crumbs, egg, onion, parsley and seasonings. Mix thoroughly.

▶ Drop by tablespoonfuls into dry crumbs and roll the mixture in the crumbs to form balls.

▶ Place in a single layer in a fry basket and fry in deep fat at 350° F. for 2 to 3 minutes or until golden brown. Drain on absorbent paper.

▶ Heat cocktail sauce and serve with oysters. Makes approximately 40 nutty oysters.

*SEAFOOD SAUCE

1 can (8 oz.) tomato sauce	¼ teaspoon liquid hot pepper sauce
¼ cup chili sauce	
¼ teaspoon garlic powder	¼ teaspoon thyme
¼ teaspoon oregano	⅛ teaspoon sugar
	Dash of basil

PREPARATION TIME: 15 MINUTES

▶ Combine all ingredients and simmer 10 to 12 minutes, stirring occasionally. Makes approximately 1 cup.

 # QUICK CANAPES

1 jar (12 oz.) herring in sour cream	1 loaf (8 oz.) party rye bread
1 large cucumber	2 tablespoons butter or margarine, softened
2 teaspoons salt	Paprika
3 cups ice water	

PREPARATION TIME: 40 MINUTES

▶ Wash cucumber and score it by running a sharp-tined fork down its length from end to end. Cut crosswise into very thin slices. Add salt to ice water and place the cucumber slices in the water. Let stand 30 minutes to crisp. Drain on absorbent paper.

continued

Spread bread with butter and overlap 2 slices of cucumber on each slice. Top cucumber with 1 large or 2 small pieces of herring.

 Sprinkle with paprika. Makes approximately 24 canapes.

SCALLOP REMOULADE* APPETIZER

1½ lb. bay scallops (or other scallops), fresh or frozen	½ teaspoon salt ¼ teaspoon thyme
1 cup water ½ cup dry white wine 2 slices onion 2 sprigs parsley	Shredded lettuce Remoulade sauce* Hard-boiled egg, optional

PREPARATION TIME: 5 MINUTES   COOKING TIME: 10 MINUTES

 Thaw scallops if frozen. Remove any remaining pieces of shell. Rinse with cold water and drain.

 In saucepan combine water, wine, onion, parsley, salt, and thyme; bring to a boil.

 Place scallops in the poaching liquid; cover, and simmer 2 to 5 minutes or until tender.

 Remove scallops from liquid; drain and chill.

 Arrange scallops on a bed of shredded lettuce in individual seafood shells or cocktail glasses.

 Spoon about 3½ tablespoons Remoulade sauce on top of each serving. Garnish with chopped hard-boiled egg, if desired. Serves six.

*REMOULADE SAUCE

2 cups mayonnaise 1 tablespoon crushed tarragon 1 tablespoon crushed capers	1 tablespoon chopped fresh parsley 1 teaspoon dry mustard 1 teaspoon anchovy paste

PREPARATION TIME: 10 MINUTES (plus chilling time).

 Mix all ingredients thoroughly.

 Chill for two hours before serving. Makes 2 cups sauce.

SEA and RANCH SALAD

1 can (6½ or 7 oz.) tuna	⅛ teaspoon pepper
¼ cup mayonnaise	1 large head iceberg lettuce
1 teaspoon dry mustard	1 avocado, sliced lengthwise
½ cup chopped celery	1 orange, peeled and sliced
¼ cup chopped walnuts	¼ cup sliced onion, separated
1 hard-cooked egg, chopped	into rings
½ teaspoon salt	Chopped parsley

PREPARATION TIME: 15 MINUTES

➧ Drain tuna.

➧ Blend mayonnaise and mustard.

➧ Combine mayonnaise mixture with tuna, celery, walnuts, egg, salt and pepper.

➧ Remove 4 large leaves from head of lettuce; shred remaining lettuce. Line each serving plate with a lettuce leaf and fill with a bed of shredded lettuce.

➧ Top with avocado slices and a scoop of tuna mixture. Garnish with orange slices and onion rings. Sprinkle with parsley. Serves four.

 # STEAMED CLAMS in WINE BROTH

3 lb. littleneck or razor clams in the shell	½ cup melted margarine or butter
½ cup dry white wine	1 lemon or lime, cut into wedges
2 tablespoons margarine or butter	

PREPARATION TIME: 10 MINUTES   COOKING TIME: 6–10 MINUTES

➧ Wash clams thoroughly with a brush under cold running water.

➧ Using a large pot with a rack or steamer, place wine and margarine in the bottom of the pot. Place rack in pot. Arrange clams on the rack and cover.

➧ Steam for 6 to 10 minutes or until clams open. Arrange clams in their shells in shallow soup bowls and pour steaming broth over clams.

➧ Serve with melted margarine and lemon wedges. Serves six.

TUNA MACARONI SALAD

1 cup cooked elbow macaroni (½ of 7-ox. pkg.)	1 can (6½ or 7 oz.) tuna, drained and flaked
1 can (8 oz.) pineapple chunks	¾ cup sliced celery
½ cup salad dressing	½ cup cubed processed American cheese
½ teaspoon curry powder, optional	½ cup chopped sweet pickle
¼ teaspoon salt	

PREPARATION TIME: 15 MINUTES (plus chilling time).

▶ Cook macaroni as directed on package. Drain and rinse well in cold water; drain again.
▶ Drain pineapple and save 2 tablespoons of syrup. Combine and mix reserved pineapple syrup, salad dressing, curry powder and salt.
▶ Pour over macaroni; mix well. Chill at least 1 hour.
▶ Add remaining ingredients; mix. Chill before serving.
▶ Serve plain or on salad greens, as you prefer. Serves six.

 # TUNA NUGGETS

2 cans (6½ or 7 oz. each) tuna	¼ teaspoon liquid hot pepper sauce
1 tablespoon lemon juice	1 cup chopped parsley
2 teaspoons horseradish	
2 pkg. (3 oz. each) cream cheese, softened	

PREPARATION TIME: 15 MINUTES

▶ Drain and flake tuna.
▶ Combine lemon juice, hot pepper sauce, horseradish and tuna and add to thoroughly softened cheese. Mix well.
▶ Portion tuna mixture with a tablespoon and shape into small balls. Roll in chopped parsley. Makes approximately 40 nuggets.

 # TUNA PUFFS*

2 cans (6½ or 7 oz. each) tuna	2 tablespoons chopped sweet pickle
1 cup finely chopped celery	Salt to taste
½ cup mayonnaise or salad dressing	Puff shells*
2 tablespoons chopped onion	

PREPARATION TIME: 20 MINUTES

continued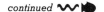

~◗

◗ Drain and flake tuna.

◗ Combine all ingredients except puff shells. Mix well.

◗ Cut tops from puff shells, and fill each shell with approximately 2 teaspoonsful of salad. Makes approximately 55 tuna puffs.

* PUFF SHELLS

½ cup boiling water	½ cup flour
¼ cup butter or margarine	2 eggs
Dash of salt	

PREPARATION TIME: 20 MINUTES   COOKING TIME: 20 MINUTES

◗ Combine water, butter and salt in a saucepan and bring to a boil.

◗ Add all flour at one time and stir vigorously until mixture leaves the sides of the pan and forms a ball. Remove from heat.

◗ Add eggs one at a time, beating thoroughly after each addition. Continue beating until a stiff dough is formed.

◗ Drop by level teaspoonful on a well-greased 15″ × 12″ cookie sheet.

◗ Bake at 450°F. for 10 minutes.

◗ Reduce heat to 350°F. and continue baking 10 minutes longer. Makes approximately 55 puff shells.

SOUPS, STEWS & CASSEROLES

 # CREAM of CRAB SOUP

1 lb. blue crab meat, fresh or frozen	2 tablespoons flour
1 vegetable bouillon cube	1 teaspoon salt
1 cup boiling water	¼ teaspoon celery salt
¼ cup chopped onion	Dash of pepper
¼ cup melted butter or cooking oil	4 drops hot pepper sauce
	1 quart milk
	Chopped parsley

PREPARATION TIME: 10 MINUTES   COOKING TIME: 15 MINUTES

Thaw crab meat if frozen. Remove any pieces of shell or cartilage.

◗ Dissolve bouillon cube in water.

◗ Cook onion in melted butter or cooking oil until tender. Blend in flour and seasonings. Add milk and bouillon gradually and cook until thickened, stirring constantly. Add crab meat; heat thoroughly. Garnish with parsley. Serves six.

CREOLE FISH with RICE

1 lb. fish fillets, fresh or frozen	½ cup chopped green pepper
1 cup chopped onion	(optional)
1 cup chopped celery	1 teaspoon garlic salt
2 tablespoons butter or	½ teaspoon chili powder
cooking oil	Dash of pepper
1 tablespoon flour	4 servings hot cooked rice
1 can (1 lb.) tomatoes	

PREPARATION TIME: 12 MINUTES   COOKING TIME: 7-10 MINUTES

▶ Thaw fish if frozen. Cut fillets into 1-inch sections. Cook rice according to directions on package.

▶ Cook onion and celery in margarine or oil in a saucepan until onion is tender (not brown). Stir in flour. Add tomatoes, green pepper and seasonings; mix well.

▶ Cover and simmer about 20 minutes. Add fish; simmer uncovered 7 to 10 minutes or until fish flakes easily when tested with a fork. Serve over hot rice. Serves four.

 ## CREOLE JAMBALAYA

1½ lb. raw, peeled, and	1 can (28 oz.) tomatoes,
de-veined shrimp, fresh or	undrained and cut up
frozen	1 can (10.5 oz.) beef broth
2 tablespoons margarine or	plus one can water
butter	1 cup uncooked long grain rice
¾ cup chopped onion	1 teaspoon sugar
½ cup chopped celery	½ teaspoon dried thyme leaves,
¼ cup chopped green pepper	crushed
1 tablespoon chopped parsley	½ teaspoon chili powder
1 clove garlic, minced	¼ teaspoon pepper
2 cups cubed, fully-cooked ham	

PREPARATION TIME: 10 MINUTES   COOKING TIME: 35-40 MINUTES

▶ Thaw shrimp if frozen.

▶ Melt margarine or butter in Dutch oven. Add onion, celery, green pepper, parsley, and garlic. Cover and cook until tender.

▶ Add remaining ingredients except shrimp. Cover, and simmer 25 minutes or until rice is tender.

▶ Add shrimp. Simmer uncovered about 5 to 10 minutes or until shrimp are cooked and the mixture has reached the desired consistency. Serves six to eight.

FISH and RICE BAKE

1 lb. fish fillets, fresh or frozen 1 can (10¾ oz.) condensed cheddar cheese soup 2 cups hot cooked rice (⅔ cups uncooked) 1 egg, beaten	2 tablespoons cooking oil or melted margarine 1 tablespoon lemon juice ½ teaspoon onion salt Paprika

PREPARATION TIME: 15 MINUTES   COOKING TIME: 5–10 MINUTES

➤ Thaw fish if frozen. Cut fillets into 1-inch sections.

➤ Prepare rice according to directions on package.

➤ Combine soup, rice and egg; mix well. Spread mixture in an even layer in a shallow 1½ quart casserole dish. Top with fish pieces. Drizzle with oil or melted margarine and lemon juice; sprinkle with salt.

➤ Cover with aluminum foil, crimping it to the edges of the dish. Bake at 350° F. for about 30 minutes.

➤ Uncover and continue to cook for 5 to 10 minutes or until hot and bubbly and fish flakes easily when tested with a fork. Sprinkle with paprika. Serves four.

 # FISH and VEGETABLE DINNER

1 lb. fish fillets, fresh or frozen 1 cup chopped onion 3 tablespoons margarine or cooking oil 2 tablespoons flour 1 teaspoon salt	Dash of pepper 1 can (13 oz.) evaporated milk 2 cups sliced boiled potatoes 1 pkg. (10 oz.) frozen peas and carrots, thawed Paprika

PREPARATION TIME: 15 MINUTES   COOKING TIME: 35–40 MINUTES

➤ Thaw fish if frozen. Cut fillets into 1-inch pieces.

➤ Cook onion in margarine or oil in a saucepan until tender, (not brown). Stir in flour, salt and pepper. Add milk; cook, stirring constantly until thick.

➤ Add vegetables; heat until bubbly. Fold in fish.

➤ Pour into a shallow 1½-quart casserole dish and cover with aluminum foil, crimping it to the edge of the dish. Bake at 350° F. for about 30 minutes; then uncover and continue cooking 5 to 10 minutes more until bubbly and fish flakes easily when tested with a fork.

➤ Sprinkle with paprika. Serves four.

FISH PORTIONS ORIENTAL

1 pkg. (12 oz.) frozen breaded fish portions	1 tablespoon soy sauce
1 can (13¼ oz.) pineapple chunks	1 tablespoon cornstarch
2 tablespoons sugar	½ teaspoon garlic salt
2 tablespoons vinegar	½ medium green pepper, cut in strips
	4 servings hot cooked rice

PREPARATION TIME: 10 MINUTES   COOKING TIME: 15 MINUTES

Heat fish portions according to directions on package.

Drain pineapple chunks; save syrup. Add water as needed to pineapple syrup to make ¾ cup liquid.

Combine liquid, sugar, vinegar, soy sauce, cornstarch and garlic salt in saucepan; mix well. Cook, stirring constantly, until sauce is thick and clear.

Add pineapple chunks and green pepper strips and heat.

Cook rice according to directions on package.

Serve fish portions on rice and spoon sauce over fish. Serves four.

FISH PORTIONS STROGANOFF CASSEROLE

1 pkg. (12 oz.) frozen breaded fish portions	1 can (10¾ oz.) condensed cream of chicken soup
2 tablespoons melted margarine or cooking oil	½ cup dairy sour cream
1 tablespoon lemon juice	½ cup milk
3 cups medium noodles (6 oz.), cooked and drained	1 teaspoon Worcestershire sauce
1 can (8½ oz.) peas and carrots, drained*	½ teaspoon onion or garlic salt
	Dash of pepper

PREPARATION TIME: 15 MINUTES   COOKING TIME: 25–30 MINUTES

Drizzle margarine or cooking oil and lemon juice over fish portions and broil as directed on package.

Cook noodles as directed on package.

Combine noodles, peas, carrots, soup, sour cream, milk, Worcestershire sauce, onion or garlic salt and pepper; mix well.

Pour into shallow 1½-quart casserole dish. Top with broiled fish portions.

Bake at 350° F. for 25 to 30 minutes or until noodle mixture is hot and bubbly. Serves four.

*You can substitute 1 package (9 oz.) of frozen peas and carrots, cooked and drained, if you prefer.

MANHATTAN FISH SOUP-STEW

1 lb. fish fillets, fresh or frozen	1 can (10 oz.) tomatoes
1½ cups sliced carrots	1 cup undiluted evaporated
1 cup water	milk
1 can (10½ oz.) condensed	1½ teaspoon onion salt
cream of potato soup	¼ teaspoon thyme
1 pkg. (9 oz.) frozen cut green	Hot biscuits, crackers or
beans, thawed	crusty bread

PREPARATION TIME: 10 MINUTES   COOKING TIME: 25 MINUTES

Thaw fish if frozen and cut into 1-inch pieces.

Combine carrot slices and water in a saucepan. Cover and simmer about 15 minutes or until carrots are almost tender.

Stir in potato soup, green beans, tomatoes, milk, salt and thyme; heat until hot and bubbly.

Add fish; cover and cook about 10 minutes or until fish flakes easily when tested with a fork and beans are cooked through.

Serve with hot biscuits, crackers or crusty bread. Makes about seven cups or four dinner-sized servings.

MEXICAN FISH with BEANS and RICE

1 lb fish fillets, fresh or frozen	1 can (1 lb.) tomatoes
1 cup chopped onion	2 tablespoons brown sugar
2 tablespoons margarine or	2 tablespoons vinegar
cooking oil	1 teaspoon prepared mustard
1 tablespoon flour	1 can (1 lb.) kidney beans,
½ teaspoon salt	drained
Dash of pepper	1½ cups hot cooked rice

PREPARATION TIME: 10 MINUTES   COOKING TIME: 25–30 MINUTES

Thaw fish if frozen. Cut fillets into 1-inch sections.

Cook onion in a saucepan in margarine or oil until tender (not brown). Stir in flour, salt and pepper. Add tomatoes, brown sugar, vinegar and mustard; mix. Simmer uncovered about 10 minutes, stirring frequently.

Add fish; simmer about 10 minutes or until fish flakes easily when tested with a fork.

Cook rice according to package directions.

Stir kidney beans into the pot of hot rice. Heat at medium until beans are hot. Serve fish over beans and rice. Serves four.

PORTUGUESE FISHERMAN STEW

2 lb. striped bass fillets or other fish fillets, fresh or frozen	1 teaspoon crushed leaf basil
	1 teaspoon crushed leaf thyme
1 tablespoon margarine or butter	¼ teaspoon crushed red pepper
	1 teaspoon salt
1 cup chopped onion	4 cups pumpkin or winter squash, cut into 1 inch cubes
1 clove garlic, crushed	
2 cans (1 lb. each) tomatoes, undrained, cut up	2 ears corn, cut crosswise into 1-inch pieces
3 cups water	

PREPARATION TIME: 15 MINUTES   COOKING TIME: 15–20 MINUTES

▶ Thaw fish if frozen. Cut into 1-inch cubes.

▶ In a large saucepan melt margarine. Add onion and garlic, and cook until onion is tender. Add tomatoes, water, basil, thyme, red pepper, salt, pumpkin, and corn. Cover and bring to a boil; simmer for 10 to 15 minutes or until pumpkin and corn are heated.

▶ Add fish and continue to cook for 5 to 10 minutes or until fish flakes easily when tested with a fork. Makes 12 cups.

SALMON CASSEROLE with CORNBREAD TOPPING

1 can (1 lb.) pink salmon	½ pkg. (1 lb. 2 oz.) corn muffin mix (or 1¾ cups dry mix)
1 can (10¾ oz.) condensed cream of mushroom soup	
1 pkg. (9 oz.) frozen cut green beans, thawed	¼ cup finely chopped green pepper (optional)
	¼ teaspoon dry mustard

PREPARATION TIME: 10 MINUTES   COOKING TIME: 20–22 MINUTES

▶ Drain salmon; save liquid.

▶ Flake salmon and distribute flakes evenly over the bottom of a shallow 1½-quart casserole dish.

▶ Combine soup, salmon liquid and green beans in a saucepan; heat. Pour soup mixture over salmon.

▶ Combine corn muffin mix, green pepper and dry mustard in a bowl. Add egg and half the amount of milk called for on the package and mix according to package directions. Spoon into 8 even mounds onto soup mixture.

▶ Bake at 400° F. for 20 to 22 minutes or until topping is browned. Serves four.

Note: You can prepare the remaining half of the corn muffin mix as directed on the package and serve with casserole.

SALMON JAMBALAYA

1 can (1 lb.) pink salmon	¾ cup uncooked rice
1 cup chopped celery	1 chicken bouillon cube
½ cup chopped onion	1 teaspoon garlic salt
2 tablespoons butter, bacon drippings, or cooking oil	½ teaspoon salt
	Dash of pepper
1½ cups water	1 bay leaf
1 can (1 lb.) tomatoes, undrained	¼ cup chopped parsley, optional

PREPARATION TIME: 10 MINUTES   COOKING TIME: 25–30 MINUTES

▶ Drain salmon; save liquid. Flake salmon.

▶ Cook celery and onion in butter, bacon drippings or oil on moderate heat until tender (not brown).

▶ Add water, tomatoes, rice, salmon liquid, bouillon cube and seasonings; stir. Cover and simmer 20 to 25 minutes or until rice is cooked thoroughly.

▶ Remove bay leaf. Fold in salmon and parsley and heat. Serves four.

 # SUPERB SEAFOOD CASSEROLE

½ lb. blue crab meat, fresh or frozen	1 teaspoon salt
	Dash of pepper
¾ lb. raw, peeled deveined shrimp, fresh or frozen	1½ cups milk
	2 tablespoons dry sherry
¼ lb. scallops, fresh or frozen	1½ cups soft bread crumbs
8 tablespoons melted butter or margarine	¼ cup finely shredded cheddar cheese
¼ cup flour	Paprika

PREPARATION TIME: 20 MINUTES   COOKING TIME: 15 MINUTES

▶ Thaw crab meat if frozen. Remove any remaining pieces of shell or cartilage.

▶ Thaw shrimp and scallops if frozen. Cut large shrimp and scallops in half and cook in 6 tablespoons melted butter or margarine over moderate heat for 4 to 6 minutes or until tender. Remove shrimp and scallops from pan.

▶ Stir flour, salt and pepper into butter or margarine. Add milk gradually and cook, stirring constantly until thickened. Stir in sherry. Fold in crab meat, shrimp and scallops.

▶ Spoon into 6 individual baking shells or ramekins.

▶ Combine bread crumbs, cheese and remaining 2 tablespoons melted butter or margarine. Sprinkle over seafood mixture.

continued 〰▶

▶ Bake at 350°F. about 15 minutes or until heated throroughly. Sprinkle with paprika. Serves six.

TUNA and NOODLES ITALIAN STYLE

1 can (9¼ oz.) tuna in oil	1 tablespoon garlic salt
1 cup sliced celery	1 teaspoon oregano
½ cup chopped onion	½ teaspoon crushed sweet basil
1 can (1 lb.) tomatoes	4 oz. medium noodles, cooked
1 can (6 oz.) tomato paste	and drained (about 3 cups
½ cup water	uncooked)
1 tablespoon sugar	¼ cup grated Parmesan cheese

PREPARATION TIME: 45 MINUTES   COOKING TIME: 30 MINUTES

▶ Drain tuna oil into a saucepan. Flake tuna.

▶ In a large saucepan, cook celery and onion in tuna oil until tender (not brown). Add tomatoes, tomato paste, water, sugar, garlic salt, oregano and basil. Cover and simmer about 30 minutes or until flavors are blended.

▶ Fold in tuna. Cook noodles according to directions on package.

▶ Spread half the noodles over bottom of a shallow 1½-quart casserole; top with half the tuna mixture and cheese. Repeat procedure using remaining ingredients.

▶ Bake at 350° F. for 30 minutes or until hot and bubbly. Serves four.

ENTRÉES

BAKED SNAPPER with SOUR CREAM STUFFING*

3 or 4 lb. dressed snapper or	Sour Cream Stuffing*
other dressed fish, fresh or	2 tablespoons melted butter or
frozen	cooking oil
1½ teaspoons salt	

PREPARATION TIME: 10 MINUTES   COOKING TIME: 40–60 MINUTES

▶ Thaw fish if frozen. Clean, wash and dry fish. Sprinkle inside and out with salt. Stuff fish loosely. Close opening with small skewers or toothpicks. Place fish on a well-greased bake-and-serve platter. Brush with melted butter or cooking oil.

▶ Bake at 350° F. for 40 to 60 minutes or until fish flakes easily when tested with a fork. Baste occasionally with melted margarine or cooking oil. Remove skewers. Serves six.

continued ▶

*SOUR CREAM STUFFING

¾ cup chopped celery	½ cup sour cream
½ cup chopped onion	¼ cup diced peeled lemon
¼ cup melted butter or cooking oil	2 tablespoons grated lemon rind
1 quart dry bread cubes	1 teaspoon paprika
	1 teaspoon salt

PREPARATION TIME: 15 MINUTES

▶ Cook celery and onion in melted butter or cooking oil until tender.

▶ Combine all ingredients and mix thoroughly. Makes approximately 1 quart stuffing.

 # BOSTON BEAN SKILLET

1½ lb. ocean perch fillets or other fish fillets, fresh or frozen	½ cup light brown sugar
1 teaspoon salt	2 tablespoons prepared mustard
¼ teaspoon pepper	1 can (1 lb.) lima beans undrained
4 slices raw bacon, diced	1 can (1 lb.) butter beans with molasses and bacon, undrained
1 cup chopped onion	
1 clove garlic, crushed	

PREPARATION TIME: 10 MINUTES   COOKING TIME: 25–30 MINUTES

▶ Thaw fish if frozen. Cut into serving-size portions. Sprinkle with salt and pepper.

▶ In a large skillet cook bacon until almost crisp. Add onion and garlic, and cook until onion is tender. Stir in brown sugar, mustard, lima beans, and butter beans. Bring mixture to a boil, and simmer for 20 to 25 minutes, stirring occasionally.

▶ Place fillets on top of beans in skillet in a single layer. Cover and simmer for 4 to 5 minutes or until fish flakes easily when tested with a fork. Makes six servings.

 # CAPE COD TURKEY with EGG SAUCE*

2 lb. cod fillets or other fish fillets, fresh or frozen	2 teaspoons dill weed
1 teaspoon salt	2 teaspoons chopped parsley
¼ teaspoon pepper	1 teaspoon crushed leaf thyme
4 tablespoons melted butter or margarine	½ teaspoon salt
	Dash of pepper
4 cups fresh bread crumbs	2 eggs, beaten
2 tablespoons grated onion	Egg Sauce*
	Sliced egg

          continued ▶

PREPARATION TIME: 10 MINUTES   COOKING TIME: 35–40 MINUTES

 Thaw fish if frozen. Sprinkle with salt and pepper. Place half the fillets in a well-greased baking dish.

 In a large bowl combine bread crumbs, 2 tablespoons margarine, onion, dill weed, parsley, thyme, salt, pepper, and eggs. Mix well. Spread on top of fillets in baking dish. Place remaining fillets on top of bread crumb stuffing; brush with 2 tablespoons melted margarine.

 Bake at 350°F., for 35 to 40 minutes or until fish flakes easily when tested with a fork. Serve fish with Egg Sauce, and garnish with a sliced egg. Makes six servings.

*EGG SAUCE

¼ cup margarine or butter	4 cups half and half
⅓ cup all-purpose flour	½ teaspoon hot pepper sauce
1 teaspoon dry mustard	5 hard-cooked eggs, chopped
1 teaspoon salt	2 tablespoons chopped parsley
⅛ teaspoon white pepper	

PREPARATION TIME: 15 MINUTES

 In a saucepan melt margarine. Stir in flour, mustard, salt, and pepper. Add half and half gradually, and cook over low heat until mixture is thick and smooth, stirring constantly. Stir in hot pepper sauce, chopped eggs, and parsley. Pour over cod fillets.

  # CLAM FETTUCINE

¼ cup soft margarine	1 can (8 oz.) tomato sauce
½ cup chopped onion	1 can (8 oz.) minced clams,
3 tablespoons flour	undrained
1 teaspoon sugar	¼ cup sliced ripe olives
1 teaspoon oregano	4 cups hot cooked seasoned
½ teaspoon salt	noodles
Dash of pepper	¼ cup grated Parmesan cheese
1 can (1 lb.) whole tomatoes,	
undrained	

PREPARATION TIME: 15 MINUTES

 Cook noodles according to package directions.

 Melt 2 tablespoons margarine in saucepan. Add onion and cook until tender (not brown).

 Combine and mix flour, sugar, oregano, salt and pepper; stir into onion mixture.

 Add tomatoes, tomato sauce, clams and olives to mixture and cook, stirring constantly until sauce thickens.

 Combine hot noodles, remaining margarine and cheese and toss until noodles are coated evenly with cheese.

 Put noodles in deep serving dish pour sauce over top. Serves four.

COD STUFFED POTATOES*

1½ lb. skinless codfish fillets or other fish fillets, fresh or frozen	1½ tablespoons grated onion
	1½ tablespoons chopped parsley
2 cups boiling water	1½ teaspoons dry mustard
1 teaspoon salt	1½ teaspoons salt
6 medium baking potatoes, baked	¼ teaspoon pepper
	Bacon drippings
1 cup hot milk	Paprika
¼ cup margarine or butter	Pork Sauce*

PREPARATION TIME: 15 MINUTES   COOKING TIME: 25 to 30 MINUTES

▶ Thaw fish if frozen.

▶ Place fish in a well-greased ten-inch fry pan. Add boiling water and salt. Cover, and simmer for 5 to 10 minutes or until fish flakes easily when tested with a fork. Remove fish from liquid, and flake. Reserve 1½ cups liquid.

▶ Cut a slice off the top of each potato; scoop out potatoes into a mixing bowl, and mash. Stir in milk, margarine, onion, parsley, mustard, salt and pepper. Stir in flaked fish.

▶ Stuff potato shells with potato-fish mixture. Drizzle with reserved bacon drippings from Pork Sauce*. Sprinkle with paprika.

▶ Bake in a moderate oven, 350°F., for 25 to 30 minutes or until hot. Serve Pork Sauce over potatoes. Makes six servings.

*PORK SAUCE

¼ lb. bacon or salt pork, minced	½ teaspoon salt
	1½ cups reserved fish liquid
¼ cup all-purpose flour	1 cup milk

PREPARATION TIME: 15 MINUTES

▶ In a small saucepan cook bacon until browned.

▶ Remove bacon; drain and reserve. Reserve 2 tablespoons bacon drippings in saucepan and reserve remaining drippings to drizzle over stuffed potatoes.

▶ To drippings in saucepan blend in flour and salt. Gradually add fish liquid and milk. Cook until thick.

▶ Stir in reserved bacon. Makes approximately 2½ cups sauce.

CREOLE BOUILLABAISSE

1 lb. red drum fillets or other fish fillets, fresh or frozen	1 cup chopped onion
1 lb. sea trout fillets or other fish fillets, fresh or frozen	½ cup chopped celery
	1 clove garlic, minced
	5 cups water
½ lb. raw, peeled, de-veined shrimp, fresh or frozen	1 can (1 lb.) tomatoes, undrained, cut up
1 pint oysters, fresh or frozen	½ cup dry white wine
1 can (6½ oz.) crabmeat, drained, cartilage removed	2 tablespoons chopped parsley
	1 tablespoon lemon juice
2 tablespoons margarine or butter	1 bay leaf
	½ teaspoon salt
2 tablespoons olive oil	¼ teaspoon saffron
¼ cup all-purpose flour	¼ teaspoon cayenne pepper

PREPARATION TIME: 25 MINUTES   COOKING TIME: 15–20 MINUTES

▶ Thaw fish and shellfish if frozen. Remove skin and bones. Cut each fish into 6 or 8 portions.

▶ In a 4-to-5-quart Dutch oven melt margarine or butter. Add olive oil and blend in flour. Cook, stirring constantly, until light brown in color.

▶ Add onion, celery, and garlic. Cook, stirring constantly, until vegetables begin to brown. Gradually stir in water, Add tomatoes, wine, parsley, lemon juice, bay leaf, salt, saffron, cayenne pepper, and about a quarter of the fish. Bring to a boil, and simmer for 20 minutes.

▶ Add remaining fish, and cook 5 to 8 minutes longer.

▶ Add shrimp, oysters, and crabmeat. Cook another 3 to 5 minutes or until all the seafood is cooked through. Serves eight.

 # DELMARVELOUS BLUEFISH*

2 lb. bluefish fillets or other fish fillets, fresh or frozen	⅓ cup melted margarine or butter
1 teaspoon salt	3 tablespoons lemon juice
½ teaspoon pepper	½ teaspoon thyme
	Mustard Sauce*

PREPARATION TIME: 10 MINUTES   COOKING TIME: 15 to 20 MINUTES

▶ Thaw fish if frozen. Cut into serving-size portions.

▶ Sprinkle with salt and pepper. Place fish in a well-greased two-quart baking dish.

▶ In a mixing bowl combine margarine, lemon juice, and thyme. Pour over fish.

▶ Bake in a moderate oven, 350° F., for 15 to 20 minutes or until fish flakes easily when tested with a fork.

▶ Serve with Mustard Sauce. Makes six servings.

continued 〰▶

*MUSTARD SAUCE

¼ cup margarine or butter	¼ teaspoon liquid hot pepper
3 tablespoons all-purpose flour	sauce
1½ tablespoons dry mustard	2 cups half and half
½ teaspoon salt	1 egg yolk, beaten

PREPARATION TIME: 15 MINUTES

 In a saucepan melt margarine.

 Blend in flour, mustard, salt, and liquid hot pepper sauce. Gradually stir in half and half. Cook until thickened, stirring constantly.

 Add a little of of the hot sauce to egg yolk; add to remaining sauce, stirring constantly. Heat until thickened.

 Serve sauce over fish. Makes approximately 2 cups sauce.

COUNTRY FISH BOIL*

2 lb. whitefish or other fish fillets, fresh or frozen	6 wedges cabbage
10 cups water	1 can (1 lb.) small whole beets
⅓ cup salt	Horseradish Sauce*
12 small red potatoes	Chopped parsley for garnish
6 medium onions, peeled	

PREPARATION TIME: 15 MINUTES   COOKING TIME: 35–40 MINUTES

 Thaw fish if frozen. Cut fillets into serving-size portions.

 In a large pot, heat water and salt to boiling. Remove a ½ inch strip of peeling around middle of potatoes. Add potatoes and onion to water; simmer 30 minutes or until tender when tested with a fork.

 Add cabbage wedges; simmer about 10 minutes until tender.

 Add fish, and simmer 3 to 4 minutes or until fish flakes easily when tested with a fork.

 Place vegetables and fish on a serving platter; keep warm.

 Add beets to water; heat. Place cooked beets on platter with other vegetables and fish. Pour on Horseradish Sauce, and garnish with finely chopped parsley. Makes six servings.

*HORSERADISH SAUCE

½ cup prepared horseradish	½ teaspoon salt
1 tablespoon all-purpose flour	1 cup half and half
¼ teaspoon paprika	

PREPARATION TIME: 10 MINUTES

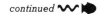
continued

▶ In a small saucepan combine horseradish, flour, paprika, and salt.
▶ Stir in half and half. Cook until thickened, stirring constantly.
Makes approximately 1½ cups sauce.

 # FISH DIVAN

1½ lb. fish fillets, fresh or frozen	1 tablespoon melted butter or margarine
2 pkg. (10 oz. each) frozen broccoli spears	½ cup skim milk
2 tablespoons flour	¼ cup grated cheddar cheese
1 teaspoon salt	1 can (1 lb.) tomatoes, chopped and well drained
¼ teaspoon pepper	¼ cup crushed cornflakes

PREPARATION TIME: 10 MINUTES   COOKING TIME: 25 MINUTES

▶ Thaw fish if frozen. Cut into serving-sized portions.
▶ Cook broccoli half as long as directed on package. Drain thoroughly
and place in a greased baking dish. Place fish over broccoli.
▶ Blend flour and seasonings into butter. Add milk gradually and
cook until thick and smooth, stirring constantly. Add cheese and stir
until melted. Stir in tomatoes.
▶ Pour sauce over fish and sprinkle with cornflakes. Bake at 350° F.
for 25 minutes or until fish flakes easily when tested with a fork.
Serves six.

 # FLOUNDER AMANDINE

2 lb. flounder fillets or other fish fillets, fresh or frozen	¼ cup melted butter or margarine
¼ cup flour	½ cup sliced almonds
1 teaspoon seasoned salt	2 tablespoons lemon juice
1 teaspoon paprika	4 to 5 drops hot pepper sauce
	1 tablespoon chopped parsley

PREPARATION TIME: 15 MINUTES   COOKING TIME: 10–12 MINUTES

▶ Thaw fillets if frozen. Cut into serving-sized portions.
▶ Combine flour, seasoned salt and paprika; mix well. Roll fish in
flour mixture. Place fish in a single layer, skin side down, in a well-
greased baking pan. Drizzle two tablespoons melted butter or
margarine over fish.
▶ Broil for 10 to 12 minutes or until fish flakes easily when tested
with a fork.

continued 〜▶

ENTRÉES

 Sauté almonds in remaining two tablespoons of melted butter or margarine until golden brown, stirring constantly. Remove from heat. Add lemon juice, hot pepper sauce and parsley; mix. Pour over fish and serve at once. Serves six.

FRIED CATFISH, ARKANSAS STYLE *

6 skinned, pan-dressed catfish or other pan-dressed fish, fresh or frozen, ½ to ¾ lb. each	¼ teaspoon pepper
	2 eggs, beaten
	2 tablespoons milk
	2 cups cornmeal
2 teaspoons salt	Fat for frying

PREPARATION TIME: 10 MINUTES   COOKING TIME: 10 MINUTES

 Thaw fish if frozen. Sprinkle both sides of fish with salt and pepper.

 Combine eggs and milk. Dip fish in mixture and roll in cornmeal.

 Place in a heavy fry pan which contains about ⅛ inch melted fat, hot but not smoking. Fry at moderate heat.

 When fish is brown on one side, turn it carefully to brown the other side. Cooking should take about 10 minutes, depending on the thickness of the fish.

 Drain on absorbent paper and serve immediately on a hot platter. Makes six servings.

Fried catfish is traditionally served with coleslaw and hush puppies.

*HUSH PUPPIES

1½ cups cornmeal	¼ cup finely chopped onion
½ cup sifted all-purpose flour	1 egg, beaten
2½ teaspoons baking powder	½ cup milk
½ teaspoon salt	Fat for deep frying

PREPARATION TIME: 20 MINUTES

 Sift dry ingredients together.

 Add remaining ingredients and stir only until blended. Drop one tablespoon at a time into deep fat, 350° F. for 3 to 4 minutes or until brown.

 Drain on absorbent paper. Makes 18.

IOWA BAKED CATFISH

6 skinned, pan-dressed catfish or other fish, fresh or frozen	1½ cups fresh bread crumbs
3 slices raw bacon, diced	1 can (8 oz.) cream-style corn
½ cup minced onion	1 can (8 oz.) whole kernel corn, drained
¼ cup minced green pepper	1 egg beaten
½ teaspoon salt	3 slices bacon, cut in half crosswise
½ teaspoon pepper	

PREPARATION TIME: 15 MINUTES   COOKING TIME: 25–30 MINUTES

▶ Thaw fish if frozen.

▶ If using catfish, remove fins. If cavity seems small for stuffing, cut tail portion open, being careful not to cut completely through. Place fish in a well-greased baking pan.

▶ In a skillet cook bacon until lightly browned. Remove bacon from skillet, reserving 2 tablespoons bacon drippings.

▶ Add to skillet onion and green pepper, and cook until vegetables are tender. Stir in salt, pepper, bread crumbs, cream-style corn, whole kernel corn, egg, and diced bacon.

▶ Stuff fish loosely with mixture. Place one half slice of bacon on top of each fish. Bake at 350° F., for 25 to 30 minutes or until fish flakes easily when tested with a fork. Makes six servings.

 # LEMON GARLIC CROAKER

2 lb. croaker fillets (or other fish fillets), fresh or frozen	1 teaspoon salt
¼ cup lemon juice	1 clove garlic, unminced
2 tablespoons butter	1½ cups cornmeal

PREPARATION TIME: 40 MINUTES   COOKING TIME: 8 MINUTES

▶ Thaw fish if frozen.

▶ Combine lemon juice, salt, and garlic in a shallow dish.

▶ Add fillets, turning them in lemon juice mixture; place them skin side up. Cover the dish and place in refrigerator to marinate for 30 minutes.

▶ Remove fish from marinade and roll it in cornmeal. Place in heavy fry pan with melted butter that's hot but not smoking. Fry at moderate heat.

▶ When fish is brown on one side, turn carefully and brown the other side.

▶ Cooking time is about 7 to 8 minutes, depending on the thickness of the fish. Drain on absorbent paper. Serve immediately on a hot platter. Serves six.

MARYLAND DEVILED CRAB

1 lb. crabmeat, fresh, frozen, or pasteurized	¾ teaspoon salt
2 tablespoons margarine or butter	¼ teaspoon hot pepper sauce
½ cup finely chopped onion	¼ teaspoon pepper
¼ cup finely chopped green pepper	Dash of cayenne (optional)
¼ cup all-purpose flour	1¼ cups half and half
1 tablespoon dry mustard	2 egg yolks, beaten
1 teaspoon Worcestershire sauce	½ cup fresh bread crumbs
	½ teaspoon paprika
	1 tablespoon margarine or butter
	Lemon wedges

PREPARATION TIME: 20 MINUTES   COOKING TIME: 15–20 MINUTES

▶ Thaw crabmeat if frozen. Remove any remaining shell or cartilage.

▶ In a large skillet melt margarine. Add onion and green pepper, and cook until vegetables are tender.

▶ Stir in flour, mustard, Worcestershire, hot pepper sauce, salt, pepper, and cayenne. Add half and half gradually. Cook over low heat until mixture has thickened, stirring constantly.

▶ Add a dash of hot sauce to egg yolks; add yolks to thickened mixture and continue stirring.

▶ Place crab mixture into 6 crab shells or ramekins.

▶ Combine bread crumbs, paprika, and margarine. Sprinkle on top of crab mixture.

▶ Bake in a moderate oven, 350° F., for 15 to 20 minutes or until mixture is hot and bread crumbs are browned.

▶ Serve with lemon wedges. Makes six servings.

NOTE: If desired, mixture may be chilled and shaped into 6 crab cakes. Dip in crumbs and fry in oil ⅛ inch deep in a skillet until golden brown on both sides.

MICHIGAN PICKELED LAKE TROUT

2 lb. lake trout fillets or other fish fillets, fresh or frozen	⅔ cup firmly packed light brown sugar
2 tablespoons margarine or butter	½ cup seedless raisins
½ cup minced onion	2 bay leaves
1½ cups apple juice	1 teaspoon salt
1 cup cider vinegar	½ cup crushed gingersnaps

PREPARATION TIME: 10 MINUTES   COOKING TIME: 8–10 MINUTES

continued 〰️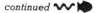

~⬖

⬖ Thaw fish if frozen. Cut fillets into serving-size portions.

⬖ Melt butter in a skillet. Add onion and cook until tender. Stir in apple juice, vinegar, brown sugar, raisins, bay leaf, and salt. Heat to boiling; simmer for 5 minutes to blend flavors.

⬖ Add fillets; cover, and simmer 3–5 minutes or until fish flakes easily when tested with a fork. Remove fish from liquid and place it in a serving dish.

⬖ Gradually add gingersnaps to liquid, stirring until smooth and thickened. Serve over fish. Makes six servings.

 # MULLET MOBILE

2 lb. mullet fillets or other fish fillets, fresh or frozen	⅛ teaspoon pepper
	Paprika
2 tablespoons melted margarine or butter	Hollandaise sauce or Béarnaise Sauce
1 teaspoon salt	(see pp. 108,110)

PREPARATION TIME: 5 MINUTES   COOKING TIME: 10–15 MINUTES

⬖ Thaw fish if frozen. Cut into six portions. Place fish in a single layer, skin side down, on a well-greased baking pan. Brush with margarine or butter and sprinkle with salt, pepper, and paprika.

⬖ Broil for 10 to 15 minutes or until fish flakes easily when tested with a fork. Fish needn't be turned during broiling. Serves six. Serve with Hollandaise or Béarnaise Sauce.

 # NEW BEDFORD WALNUT FRIED FLOUNDER

2 lb. flounder fillets or other fish fillets, fresh or frozen	1 teaspoon marjoram leaves
	½ teaspoon crushed leaf thyme
1 teaspoon salt	1 cup all-purpose flour
¼ teaspoon pepper	2 eggs, beaten
1½ cups fresh bread crumbs	⅓ cup margarine or butter
1½ cups ground walnuts	⅓ cup cooking oil
1½ teaspoons crushed rosemary	Lemon wedges

PREPARATION TIME: 15 MINUTES   COOKING TIME: 8–10 MINUTES

⬖ Thaw fish if frozen. Sprinkle with salt and pepper.

⬖ Combine bread crumbs, walnuts, rosemary, marjoram, and thyme.

⬖ Roll fillets in flour, dip in egg, and roll in crumb mixture.

continued ~⬖

〰️▶️

▶️ Heat margarine and oil in a fry pan until hot, but not smoking. Place fish in pan and fry at a moderate heat for 4 to 5 minutes or until browned. Turn carefully and fry 4 to 5 minutes longer or until fish is browned and flakes easily when tested with a fork.

▶️ Drain on absorbent paper. Serve with lemon wedges. Makes six servings.

 # OUTER BANKS STUFFED SPANISH MACKEREL*

2 to 4 lb. dressed Spanish mackerel or other dressed fish, fresh or frozen ½ teaspoon salt	¼ teaspoon pepper Vegetable stuffing* 2 tablespoons melted butter or margarine

PREPARATION TIME: 5 MINUTES   COOKING TIME: 30–45 MINUTES

▶️ Thaw fish if frozen. Wash and dry cleaned fish.

▶️ Sprinkle inside and out with salt and pepper. Place on a well-greased bake-and-serve platter. Stuff fish, brush with margarine.

▶️ Bake at 350° F. for 30 to 45 minutes or until fish flakes easily when tested with a fork. Serves six.

*VEGETABLE STUFFING .

½ cup margarine or butter 1½ cups chopped onion 1 cup chopped celery 1 cup chopped fresh mushrooms ½ cup chopped green pepper	1 clove garlic, minced 2 tomatoes, peeled, seeded, and chopped 3 cups soft bread crumbs ½ teaspoon salt

PREPARATION TIME: 10 MINUTES

▶️ Melt margarine or butter in saucepan.

▶️ Add onion, celery, mushrooms, green pepper, and garlic; cover and cook until tender.

▶️ Combine all ingredients and mix well. Makes 3½ cups stuffing.

 # OVEN-FRIED BLUEFISH

2 lb. bluefish fillets or other fish fillets, fresh or frozen 1¼ teaspoons salt ¼ teaspoon pepper 1 cup instant mashed potato flakes	1 pkg. (7/10 oz.) cheese garlic salad dressing mix 1 egg, beaten ¼ cup butter or margarine Paprika

PREPARATION TIME: 10 MINUTES   COOKING TIME: 10–12 MINUTES

continued 〰️▶️

〰️ ▶

▶ Thaw fish if frozen. Skin fillets and cut into serving-sized portions. Season fish with salt and pepper.
▶ Combine potato flakes and salad dressing mix.
▶ Dip fish into beaten egg and roll in potato mixture. Place fish in a single layer in a well-greased bake-and-serve platter. Pour melted butter over fish. Sprinkle with paprika.
▶ Bake at 500° F. for 10 to 12 minutes or until fish flakes easily when tested with a fork. Serves six.

PENOBSCOT BAY FISH PUDDING

2 cans (3¾ or 4 oz. each) Maine sardines	1½ cups half and half
4 cups sliced boiled potatoes	2 eggs, beaten
½ teaspoon salt	1 tablespoon all-purpose flour
⅛ teaspoon pepper	½ cup shredded cheddar cheese
2 tablespoons minced onion	Tomatoes, sliced thin

PREPARATION TIME: 15 MINUTES   COOKING TIME: 35–40 MINUTES

▶ Drain sardines. Cut in half lengthwise.
▶ Place a layer of sliced potatoes in a well-greased 1½ -quart round casserole. Arrange sardines over potatoes. Top with remaining potatoes.
▶ Combine half and half, eggs, flour, salt, and pepper. Pour over potatoes and sardines. Bake in moderate oven, 350° F., for 35 to 40 minutes or until a knife inserted near center comes out clean.
▶ Sprinkle casserole with cheese; return casserole to oven and leave it there until cheese melts. Garnish with tomato slices. Makes six servings.

SANDY BOG FILLETS*

2 lb. haddock fillets or other fish fillets, fresh or frozen	½ cup sliced onion
	1 bay leaf
4 cups apple juice	4 peppercorns
1 rib celery, cut into 1-inch lengths	1 teaspoon salt
	Cranberry sauce*

PREPARATION TIME: 10 MINUTES   COOKING TIME: 15 MINUTES

continued 〰️▶

ENTRÉES

〜🐟

🐟 Thaw fillets if frozen. Cut into serving-size portions.

🐟 In a 10-inch skillet combine apple juice, onion, celery, bay leaf, peppercorns, and salt. Heat to boiling. Simmer for 10 minutes to blend flavors.

🐟 Add fish, and poach 4 to 5 minutes or until fish flakes easily when tested with a fork. Carefully place fish on a hot platter.

🐟 Reserve poaching liquid; strain. Pour cranberry sauce over fish. Makes six servings.

*CRANBERRY SAUCE

Reserved poaching liquid	¼ cup lemon juice
2 cups fresh cranberries	¾ teaspoon cinnamon
¼ cup sugar	

PREPARATION TIME: 5 MINUTES   COOKING TIME: 10 MINUTES

🐟 Cook poaching liquid over medium heat until it is reduced to one cup.

🐟 Add cranberries, sugar, lemon juice, and cinnamon to poaching liquid.

🐟 Cook over moderate heat approximately 5 minutes or until cranberry skins burst. Makes approximately 2 cups sauce.

SAN PEDRO TUNA OMELET

2 cans (6½ or 7 oz. each) tuna, drained and flaked	2 tablespoons flour
	¼ cup water
2 cups half-and-half	¼ cup margarine or butter
2 tablespoons sliced green onion	12 eggs
½ teaspoon thyme	Dash of pepper
2 teaspoons salt	1½ cups shredded cheddar
6–8 drops hot pepper sauce	cheese

PREPARATION TIME: 20 MINUTES   COOKING TIME: 15 MINUTES

🐟 In a saucepan, heat tuna, half-and-half, onion, thyme, ½ teaspoon salt and hot pepper sauce until the mixture is hot.

🐟 Blend flour and water together in a separate bowl and add to sauce, stirring constantly. Cook until thick.

🐟 For each omelet beat 2 eggs, ¼ teaspoon salt and a dash of pepper together.

🐟 Heat 2 teaspoons margarine in a small omelet pan until margarine sizzles. Pour egg mixture into omelet pan. When eggs are partially cooked, run a spatula around the edge, lifting slightly to allow uncooked egg to flow underneath.

continued 〜🐟

🐟 When omelet is almost done, sprinkle ¼ cup cheese on top and continue to cook until cheese melts.

🐟 Remove omelet and place on a hot platter. Repeat procedure until you have made 6 omelets.

🐟 Place ½ cup tuna mixture atop one side of each omelet. Fold omelets in half. Serves six.

 # SEA TROUT MEUNIÈRE *

2 lb. sea trout fillets or other fish fillets, fresh or frozen	1 teaspoon salt
	¼ teaspoon cayenne pepper
1 egg, beaten	Meunière Sauce*
2 tablespoons milk	Chopped parsley
1 cup all-purpose flour	Fat for deep frying

PREPARATION TIME: 10 MINUTES   COOKING TIME: 3 to 5 MINUTES

🐟 Thaw fish if frozen. Skin fillets and cut into six portions.

🐟 Combine egg and milk. In a separate container mix together flour, salt, and cayenne. Dip fish into egg mixture and then roll in flour.

🐟 Allow a few minutes for fillets to dry. Place in a single layer in a fry basket.

🐟 Fry in deep fat, 350° F., for 3 to 5 minutes or until fish are browned and flake easily when tested with a fork.

🐟 Drain on absorbent paper; keep fillets warm while remaining fish is frying.

🐟 To serve, place each fillet on a heated plate and pour about ½ tablespoon Meunière sauce over each. Sprinkle with chopped parsley. Serves six.

*MEUNIÈRE SAUCE

½ cup margarine or butter	1 tablespoon lemon juice

PREPARATION TIME: 5 MINUTES

🐟 In a small heavy saucepan melt margarine over low heat.

🐟 Continue heating until margarine turns light brown. Add lemon juice. Makes ½ cup sauce.

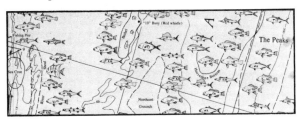

SOURDOUGH FRIED FISH
with BLUEBERRY SAUCE*

SOURDOUGH STARTER

1 pkg. active dry yeast	2 tablespoons sugar
1 qt. lukewarm water	4 cups all-purpose flour

PREPARATION TIME: 10 MINUTES (plus several days' standing time)

► In a large crock or mixing bowl, soften yeast in water.

► Add sugar and flour. Beat until ingredients are blended.

► Cover and let rise. Let stand at room temperature for several days to develop slightly sour flavor; then refrigerate.

► As starter is used, add equal amounts of flour and water to replace the quantities used. The starter will need one additional cup of flour about once a week if not used and must be stirred daily.

SOURDOUGH FRIED FISH

STEP 1

½ cup sourdough starter	1 cup lukewarm water
1¼ cups all-purpose flour	

PREPARATION TIME: 5 MINUTES (plus standing time)

► If you'll be using frozen fish, place it in the refrigerator now to thaw overnight.

► Mix sourdough starter, flour and water and let stand in refrigerator overnight.

STEP 2

¼ cup milk or cream	1 tablespoon vegetable oil
1 egg, beaten	½ teaspoon baking soda
1 tablespoon sugar	½ teaspoon salt

PREPARATION TIME: 20 MINUTES

► Combine all ingredients in a bowl and stir into refrigerated batter from step 1. Let it stand and bubble for 10 minutes.

STEP 3

2 lb. lingcod fillets, or other	¼ teaspoon pepper
thick fish fillets	½ cup flour
(thawed if frozen)	Fat for frying
1 teaspoon salt	Blueberry Sauce*

PREPARATION TIME: 10 MINUTES   COOKING TIME: 8 MINUTES

continued 〰️ ►

〰▶

▶ Cut fish into serving-sized portions and sprinkle with salt and pepper; then coat with flour.

▶ Dip fish in batter from step 2. Fry coated fish in a large, deep skillet in fat approximately 2 inches deep, turning once until both sides are brown and fish flakes easily when tested with a fork. Drain on absorbent paper and serve with hot blueberry sauce. Serves six.

*BLUEBERRY SAUCE

2 cups blueberries	2 tablespoons lemon juice
½ cup water	1 teaspoon cornstarch
¼ to ⅓ cup sugar	1 tablespoon water
2-inch cinnamon stick	

PREPARATION TIME: 15 MINUTES

▶ In a saucepan, combine blueberries, water, sugar and cinnamon. Heat to simmering, stirring until sugar is dissolved. Simmer 5 minutes. Stir in lemon juice.

▶ Blend cornstarch and water together and add to sauce, stirring constantly.

▶ Heat to boiling, stirring constantly. Boil 2 minutes. Makes 1¾ cups sauce.

 # SPICY PAN-FRIED FISH

3 lb. fish fillets or small pan-dressed fish	½ teaspoon pepper
	½ teaspoon celery salt
1 cup buttermilk	¼ teaspoon dry mustard
1 cup yellow corn meal	¼ teaspoon onion powder
½ cup flour	Cooking oil
1½ teaspoons paprika	Lemon wedges
1 teaspoon salt	

PREPARATION TIME: 10 MINUTES   COOKING TIME: 4-5 MINUTES

▶ Cut fish into serving-sized portions.

▶ Combine dry ingredients.

▶ Dip fish in buttermilk, then in dry mixture.

▶ Heat oil to 365° F. Fry fish 4 to 5 minutes or until it flakes easily when tested with a fork.

▶ Drain on absorbent paper. Serve with lemon wedges and tartar sauce. Serves six to eight.

SVENSKIE SMELT FRY*

20 medium smelt (about 1 lb.)	3 tablespoons cooking oil
1 can (2 oz.) anchovy fillets	4 slices toasted rye bread, crusts removed
¼ teaspoon salt	Svenskie Sauce*
⅛ teaspoon pepper	Lemon twists and dill sprigs for garnish
½ cup all-purpose flour	
3 tablespoons butter or margarine	

PREPARATION TIME: 15 MINUTES   COOKING TIME: 10 MINUTES

▶ Drain anchovies, reserving oil to use in Svenskie Sauce. Cut anchovies in half lengthwise. Place one half anchovy inside each fish. Sprinkle fish with salt and pepper, and roll in flour.

▶ In a large skillet, heat butter and cooking oil to a moderate temperature. Add fish and fry until crisp.

▶ Place 5 fish on each slice of rye toast. Spoon sauce over smelt. Garnish with lemon twists and dill sprigs. Serves four.

*SVENSKIE SAUCE

Reserved anchovy oil	1 egg yolk, beaten
2 tablespoons minced onion	1 tablespoon lemon juice
1½ tablespoons flour	1 tablespoon chopped fresh dill (or ½ teaspoon dried dillweed)
½ teaspoon salt	
1⅓ cups half and half	

PREPARATION TIME: 15 MINUTES

▶ In a saucepan, cook onion in anchovy oil over moderate heat until tender. Blend in flour and salt. Gradually stir in half and half. Cook until thickened, stirring constantly.

▶ Add a little of the heated sauce mixture to egg yolk; add yolk to remaining sauce in pan, stirring constantly. Heat until thickened. Add lemon juice and dill. Makes 1⅓ cups sauce.

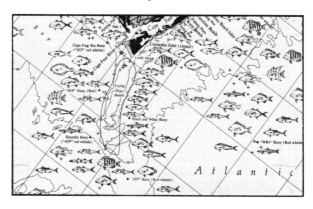

TEXAS FILLETS

2 lb. fish fillets	3 tablespoons chopped green
2 tablespoons lemon juice	onion
½ cup grated Parmesan cheese	¼ teaspoon salt
¼ cup margarine or butter	Dash liquid hot pepper sauce
3 tablespoons mayonnaise	

PREPARATION TIME: 5 MINUTES   COOKING TIME: 8 MINUTES

 Place fillets in a single layer on a well-greased baking platter. Brush with lemon juice.

Combine remaining ingredients.

Broil fish for 6 minutes or until fish flakes easily when tested with a fork. Remove from heat and spread with cheese mixture.

Broil 2 more minutes or until lightly browned. Serves six.

WHITING, GLOUCESTER STYLE

2 lb. whiting fillets or other fish fillets, fresh or frozen	¼ cup chopped onion
½ teaspoon salt	2 tablespoons chopped green pepper
½ teaspoon garlic salt	1 clove garlic, crushed
¼ teaspoon pepper	1 can (1 lb.) tomatoes, undrained, cut up
1 cup all-purpose flour	¼ teaspoon thyme
¼ cup margarine or butter	3 slices (1 oz. each) cheese, cut in half
¼ cup cooking oil	
2 tablespoons margarine or butter	

PREPARATION TIME: 20 MINUTES   COOKING TIME: 8–10 MINUTES

Thaw fish if frozen. Divide into serving-size portions. Sprinkle with salt, garlic salt, and pepper. Roll fish in flour.

Heat ¼ cup margarine and ¼ cup cooking oil in frying pan until hot, but not smoking. Place fish in pan and fry at a moderate heat for 4 to 5 minutes until browned. Turn carefully and fry for 4 to 5 minutes longer or until fish is browned and flakes easily when tested with a fork.

In a saucepan melt 2 tablespoons margarine. Add onion, green pepper, and garlic, and cook until tender.

Add tomatoes and thyme. When sauce is hot, pour into a baking dish. Place fish on top of sauce. Arrange cheese on top of fish. Bake at 350° F., for 8 to 10 minutes or until cheese melts. Makes six servings.

ENTRÉES

WINNIBIGOSHISH
WALLEYE and WILD RICE*

2 lb. walleye pike fillets or other fish fillets, fresh or frozen 1 teaspoon salt ¼ teaspoon pepper 3 slices raw bacon, diced 1 cup chopped fresh mushrooms (about ¼ lb.)	¼ cup minced onion ¼ cup minced celery 2 cups cooked wild rice ½ teaspoon salt 2 tablespoons melted margarine or butter Mushroom-Walnut Sauce*

PREPARATION TIME: 15 MINUTES   COOKING TIME: 15 MINUTES

▶ Thaw fish if frozen.

▶ Cut fillets into serving-size portions and season with 1 teaspoon salt and ¼ teaspoon pepper.

▶ In a skillet cook bacon until lightly browned. Add mushrooms, onion, and celery; cook until tender. Stir in rice and salt.

▶ Place fillets in a well-greased baking pan. Place approximately ½ cup rice mixture on top of each fillet. Drizzle melted margarine over the rice.

▶ Bake at 350° F., for about 20 minutes or until fish flakes easily when tested with a fork. Serve with Mushroom-Walnut Sauce. Makes six servings.

*MUSHROOM-WALNUT SAUCE

3 tablespoons margarine or butter 1 tablespoon minced onion 1 cup sliced mushrooms (about ¼ lb.) 3 tablespoons flour	½ teaspoon dry mustard ½ teaspoon salt ¼ teaspoon thyme 2 cups half and half ¼ cup toasted walnuts

PREPARATION TIME: 10 MINUTES

▶ Melt butter in a saucepan. Add onion and mushrooms, and cook until tender.

▶ Stir in flour, mustard, salt, and thyme. Gradually stir in half and half. Cook over medium heat until thickened, stirring constantly.

▶ Stir in nuts. Serve sauce over fish and wild rice. Makes approximately 2½ cups sauce.

BROILED FILLETS
MEXICALI

2 lb. sheepshead fillets or other fish fillets	1 teaspoon paprika
2 tablespoons cooking oil	½ teaspoon chili powder
2 tablespoons soy sauce	½ teaspoon garlic powder
2 tablespoons Worcestershire sauce	Dash of hot pepper sauce
	Lemon wedges

PREPARATION TIME: 5 MINUTES

▶ Cut fillets into serving-size portions and place in a single layer in a well-greased baking dish.

▶ Combine remaining ingredients and pour over fillets.

▶ Broil approximately 10 minutes or until fish flakes easily when tested with a fork.

▶ Baste once with natural juices during broiling. Serve with lemon wedges. Serves six.

Approximately 115 calories per serving.

CHEF'S SALAD
CHESAPEAKE*

1 can (12 oz.) blue crab meat or other crab meat, fresh, frozen, or pasteurized	6 large lettuce leaves
1 package (10 oz.) frozen asparagus spears	Lemon-Caper dressing*
	3 hard-boiled eggs, sliced
	Paprika

PREPARATION TIME: 10 MINUTES

▶ Thaw crab meat if frozen. Drain, and remove any shell or cartilage. Flake the meat.

▶ Cook asparagus spears according to directions on the package; drain and chill.

▶ Place 3 asparagus spears in each lettuce leaf. Place about ⅓ cup crab meat on asparagus. Cover with approximately 2 tablespoons Lemon-Caper dressing. Top with 3 slices of egg and sprinkle with paprika. Serves six.

Approximately 130 calories per serving.

continued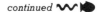

*LEMON-CAPER DRESSING

½ cup low-calorie mayonnaise-type salad dressing	½ teaspoon prepared mustard
	½ teaspoon Worcestershire sauce
1 tablespoon capers, drained	2 drops hot pepper sauce
1 tablespoon lemon juice	

PREPARATION TIME: 10 MINUTES (excluding chilling time)

 Combine all ingredients and chill. Makes approximately ⅔ cup dressing.

 # COD CURRY

2 lb. cod fillets or other fish fillets, fresh or frozen	1 teaspoon curry powder
1 cup thinly sliced celery	1 teaspoon salt
1 cup thinly sliced onion	Dash of pepper
1 tablespoon melted fat or oil	¾ cup skim milk
	Paprika

PREPARATION TIME: 10 MINUTES   COOKING TIME: 25-30 MINUTES

 Thaw fish if frozen. Skin fillets and place in a single layer in a greased baking dish.

 Cook the celery and onion in fat for 5 minutes. Stir in seasoning and milk, and spread over fillets.

 Bake at 350°F. for 25 to 30 minutes or until fish flakes easily when tested with a fork. Sprinkle with paprika. Serves six.

Approximately 140 calories per serving.

 # COUNTRY CRAB SOUP

1 lb. blue crab meat, fresh or pasteurized	2 cups chicken broth, fat skimmed
⅓ cup finely chopped onion	12 oz. low-sodium tomato juice
¼ cup finely chopped celery	1 teaspoon basil
¼ cup finely chopped green pepper	1 teaspoon salt
	¼ teaspoon thyme
1 clove garlic, minced	¼ teaspoon cayenne pepper
2 tablespoons dietetic margarine	10 oz. frozen mixed vegetables

PREPARATION TIME: 10 MINUTES   COOKING TIME: 10 MINUTES

continued

Remove shell or cartilage from crab meat.

 In a three-quart saucepan cook onion, celery, green pepper, and garlic in margarine until tender but not brown.

 Add broth, tomato juice, basil, salt, thyme, and pepper. Bring to a boil.

 Reduce heat, and simmer for 10 minutes.

 Add mixed vegetables. Cover; simmer for 10 minutes.

 Add crab meat and continue cooking until vegetables are tender and crab meat is heated.

 Serves six.

Approximately 150 calories per serving.

FLOUNDER in WINE SAUCE

2 lb. flounder fillets or other fish fillets, fresh or frozen	2 tablespoons flour
1½ teaspoons salt	2 tablespoons melted butter or margarine
Dash of pepper	½ cup skim milk
3 tomatoes, sliced	⅓ cup dry white wine
½ teaspoon salt	½ teaspoon crushed basil
Additional dash of pepper	Chopped parsley

PREPARATION TIME: 15 MINUTES   COOKING TIME: 25–30 MINUTES

 Thaw fillets if frozen.

 Skin fillets and sprinkle on both sides with 1½ teaspoons salt and dash of pepper. Place fillets in a single layer in a greased baking dish. Arrange tomatoes on top of fillets. Sprinkle with remaining salt and pepper.

 In a saucepan blend flour into melted butter. Add milk gradually and cook over medium heat until sauce is thick and smooth, stirring constantly.

Remove from heat; stir in wine and basil. Pour sauce over tomatoes and fish.

 Bake at 350° F. for 25 to 30 minutes or until fish flakes easily when tested with a fork

 Sprinkle with parsley. Serves six.

Approximately 180 calories per serving.

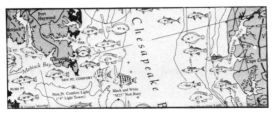

HEARTY HALIBUT

2 lb. halibut steaks or other fish steaks, fresh or frozen	3 tablespoons chopped pimiento
⅔ cup thinly sliced onion	½ cup dry white wine
1½ cups chopped fresh mushrooms	2 tablespoons lemon juice
⅓ cup chopped tomato	1 teaspoon salt
¼ cup chopped green pepper	¼ teaspoon dill weed
¼ cup chopped parsley	⅛ teaspoon pepper
	Lemon wedges

PREPARATION TIME: 10 MINUTES   COOKING TIME: 25–30 MINUTES

▶ Thaw fish if frozen. Cut steaks into serving-size portions.
▶ Arrange onion slices on the bottom of a greased baking dish, and place fish steaks on top.
▶ Combine remaining vegetables and spread over top of fish.
▶ Combine wine, lemon juice, and seasoning, and pour over vegetables.
▶ Bake at 350° F. for 25 to 30 minutes or until fish flakes easily when tested with a fork.
▶ Serve with lemon wedges. Serves six.

Approximately 230 calories per serving.

 # KEY LIME MULLET

2 lb. mullet fillets or any other fish fillets, fresh or frozen	¼ cup lime juice
	3 tablespoon butter or margarine
1 teaspoon salt	Paprika
Dash of pepper	Lime wedges

PREPARATION TIME: 35 MINUTES   COOKING TIME: 8–10 MINUTES

▶ Thaw fish if frozen. Skin fillets and cut into serving-size portions. Place fish in a single layer in a shallow baking dish. Sprinkle with salt and pepper.
▶ Pour lime juice over fish and let stand for 30 minutes, turning once.
▶ Remove fish and reserve juice. Place fish on a well-greased broiler pan.
▶ Combine butter and juice. Brush fish with this mixture and sprinkle with paprika.
▶ Broil 8 to 10 minutes or until fish flakes easily when tested with a fork. Serve with lime wedges. Serves six.

Approximately 130 calories per serving.

OLD-FASHIONED FISH DINNER

1 lb. redfish fillets or other thick fillets, fresh or frozen	½ teaspoon oregano
6 chicken bouillon cubes	⅛ teaspoon pepper
1 cup thinly sliced peeled carrots	1 can (4½ oz.) sliced mushrooms, undrained
2 medium onions, sliced into eighths	1 peeled tomato, cut into eight wedges
2 tablespoons cornstarch	2 tablespoons sliced Spanish olives
2 cups broccoli pieces	¼ cup cold water
½ teaspoon basil	

PREPARATION TIME: 15 MINUTES   COOKING TIME: 5–8 MINUTES

▶ Thaw fish if frozen. Cut into 2-inch chunks.

▶ Combine 6 cups hot water, bouillon cubes, carrots, and onion in a large stew pot or Dutch oven. Bring to a boil.

▶ Cover, and cook just until carrots are tender.

▶ Combine cornstarch and ¼ cup cold water. Add to hot liquid, stirring constantly until cornstarch is cooked.

▶ Add broccoli, basil, oregano, and pepper; cook uncovered for 5 minutes.

▶ Add fish chunks, mushrooms, tomatoes, and olives. Stir carefully to mix.

▶ Cover, and cook 5 to 8 minutes or until fish flakes. Makes about 10 one-cup servings.

Approximately 121 calories per serving.

 # SAVORY BAKED HADDOCK

2 lb. haddock fillets or other fish fillets, fresh or frozen	½ cup soft bread crumbs
2 teaspoons lemon juice	2 tablespoons chopped parsley
Dash of pepper	¾ cup thinly sliced onion
6 slices raw bacon	2 tablespoons bacon fat

PREPARATION TIME: 15 MINUTES   COOKING TIME: 25–30 MINUTES

▶ Thaw fish if frozen. Skin fillets and place in a single layer in a greased baking dish. Sprinkle with lemon juice and pepper.

▶ Fry bacon until crisp. Remove from fat and crumble into bowl with bread crumbs and parsley.

▶ Cook onion in bacon fat until tender. Spread onion over fish and sprinkle crumb mixture on top of onion.

▶ Bake at 350°F. for 25 to 30 minutes or until fish flakes easily when tested with a fork. Serves six.

Approximately 170 calories per serving.

THE CHEF RECOMMENDS

A "specialty of the house" is a dish
that has evolved slowly and withstood
the test of time. It is usually the product of a recipe that has been altered
and refined over the years—new
ingredients have been added, tasted,
and incorporated into the recipe per-
manently or rejected. In the case of fine
restaurants, different chefs add their
own individual touches to the dish. The
final product is a synthesis of different
palates, tastes and ingredients, blended
to create one truly outstanding dish.
Most dishes of this type, with their own
history and character, can be created in
your own home. And there is ample
opportunity for experimentation and
refinement. Seafood lends itself especially well to this process because of its
versatility; and some of the country's
leading restaurants offer seafood
dishes as their "specialty of the house."

Restaurant meals carry with them a sense of festivity and glamour. In *The Chef Recommends...*, leading restaurants throughout the country have provided recipes enabling you to prepare famous seafood specialities in your own kitchen.

Although many of the restaurants featured are noted for more than their seafood, each considers seafood a "specialty of the house." Some of the country's most skilled and creative chefs have shared their most popular recipes here. With these recipes, you can recreate "Breakfast at Brennan's," a New Orleans tradition, taste authentic crab soup as prepared at New York City's *Maryland Crab House* or sample an entrée from San Francisco's historic *Tadich Grill.*

Each recipe is accompanied by a brief description of the restaurant, including the type of cuisine it offers, a brief history, owner's name, reservations policy and days open.

The recipes include appetizers, soups, chowders, quiches, and simple and complex entrées. Each has been reproduced essentially as the restaurant supplied it, with the tips for serving included by the chefs.

Although these restaurant recipes are somewhat more eclectic than those featured in *Cooking The Catch,* they are not difficult to prepare at home. Each has been assigned an estimated preparation and cooking time to give you a general idea of how much time to allot for the preparation of each dish. The instruction portion of each recipe is divided into short paragraphs. Each new paragraph, indicated by a small black fish near the left-hand margin, signals the beginning of a new step or procedure.

INDEX

Brennan's

317 Royal, Street New Orleans, LA 70130 (504) 525-9713

Brennan's was founded in 1946 by Owen Brennan, an Irishman who wanted to create a restaurant blending fine French cuisine with Louisiana's native creole creativity. Since most New Orleans restaurants at that time were open only for lunch and dinner, Brennan decided to open earlier and beat the competition. A best-selling book of the day entitled *Dinner at Antoine's* inspired Brennan to call his innovation *Breakfast at Brennan's*. The elaborate menu, featuring well-known standard dishes in addition to inventions of the Brennan family and staff, turned the breakfast into a New Orleans tradition. On an average day, Brennan's serves more than 1,000 breakfasts and 400 dinners.

Owners: Maude, Owen, Theodore and James Brennan. Reservations suggested. Open seven days.

EGGS ST. CHARLES

4 trout fillets, halved	¼ teaspoon pepper
1¼ cups milk	Vegetable oil for frying
1½ cups flour	16 poached eggs
1 teaspoon salt	Brennan's hollandaise sauce*

PREPARATION TIME: 20 MINUTES   COOKING TIME: 5 MINUTES

▶ Soak the fillets in milk for about 5 minutes, then roll them in flour, salt and pepper, coating evenly.

▶ Deep- or shallow-fry the fillets in hot oil (375° F.) for about 5 minutes or until crisp and brown. Remove from the oil with tongs, allowing the excess oil to drain off. Place fillets on paper towels to drain.

▶ Poach the eggs.

▶ Place 1 piece of trout on each of 8 heated serving plates, top each with two poached eggs, and cover evenly with hollandaise sauce.

*HOLLANDAISE SAUCE

8 large egg yolks	1 teaspoon salt
4 tablespoons lemon juice	¼ teaspoon cayenne pepper
1½ lb. hot melted butter, clarified	

PREPARATION TIME: 15 MINUTES

▶ Place egg yolks and lemon juice in a mixing bowl. (It's best to set the bowl on top of a warm stove as you work to keep the mixture warm.) Beat yolks and juice briefly with a whisk. Slowly pour in the hot melted butter, beating briskly and constantly as you pour.

▶ When the sauce begins to thicken, sprinkle in salt and cayenne pepper. Continue to beat while adding in the rest of the butter.

▶ Beat the sauce until it reaches a thick consistency. Leave the bowl on the stove to keep it warm until you need it, or set it in a basin of warm water.

 continued

SHRIMP CREOLE BRENNAN

½ cup butter	½ teaspoon black pepper
1 cup green pepper, chopped	¼ teaspoon cayenne
3 cups white onions, chopped	3 bay leaves, broken up
1 cup celery, chopped	1½ teaspoons leaf thyme
2 tablespoons garlic, very	4 or 5 cups water
finely chopped	4 lb. raw shrimp, peeled
¾ cup flour	and deveined (7 or 8
3 cups whole canned tomatoes	lb. if bought in the shell)
2 teaspoons salt	

PREPARATION TIME: 25 MINUTES

In a large heavy saucepan, melt butter over medium heat. Add green pepper, onions, celery and garlic. Cook, stirring frequently, until vegetables begin to brown.

Quickly stir in flour and continue cooking, stirring constantly, until the mixture is a rich light brown color. Add tomatoes and mash them in with the back of a large spoon. Cook for 3 minutes stirring to blend ingredients thoroughly.

Add salt, pepper, cayenne, bay leaves and thyme. Stir to blend well, then turn the heat to high and gradually add water. After you've added 4 cups, allow the sauce to boil, then lower the heat and simmer for 10 minutes, stirring frequently. If the sauce appears too thick when the 10 minutes are nearly up, add the 5th cup of water.

Add the shrimp and bring sauce to a boil again. Lower heat slightly and cook until shrimp are tender, about 5 to 7 minutes. Serves eight.

Brennan's serves its shrimp creole with boiled rice.

OYSTER SOUP BRENNAN

1 cup butter	4 dozen large shucked oysters
2 cups celery, finely chopped	12 cups oyster water (oyster
1 cup green onions, finely	liquid plus sufficient water
chopped	to make 12 cups
1¼ cups flour	4 bay leaves
2 tablespoons garlic, finely	1 teaspoon thyme
chopped	2 teaspoons salt
	1 teaspoon white pepper

PREPARATION TIME: 35 MINUTES

Melt the butter in a heavy 6-quart saucepan over medium heat.

Sauté the celery and green onions in melted butter until tender, not browned, stirring frequently. Slowly stir in flour. Cook for 5 minutes over low heat, stirring constantly.

Add remaining ingredients and simmer for 20 minutes. Remove bay leaves and discard. Serves eight.

BOOKBINDERS

215 South 15th Street Philadelphia, PA 19102 (215) 515-1137

The first Bookbinders was founded by Samuel Bookbinder 90 years ago. He ran the restaurant from 125 Walnut Street with the help of his brother and sister until 1944, when the restaurant was sold. In 1935, however, Samuel's son Coleman, a manager at his father's restaurant, left the original Bookbinders to start his own restaurant at 215 South 15th Street. Although the old original Bookbinders still exists, descendents of Samuel Bookbinder today run Bookbinder's Seafood House, carrying on Samuel and Coleman's tradition of good seafood served in a no-frills fashion.

Owners: Samuel C. Bookbinder, Jr. and Richard C. Bookbinder. Reservations suggested. Open seven days.

BAY SCALLOPS PROVENÇALE with FETTUCINE

¾ lb. of fresh bay scallops (small)	2 tablespoons fresh chives, chopped
2 cups fish broth	½ pint heavy cream
¾ lb. fettucine	½ pint ricotta cheese
1 large tomato, peeled, seeded and seasoned to taste with salt and pepper	½ cup Romano cheese, grated
	Pinch of salt and pepper
5 or 6 basil leaves, chopped	¼ teaspoon granulated garlic

PREPARATION TIME: 25 MINUTES

Poach scallops in fish broth until slightly firm. Remove from heat and keep warm.

Cook pasta according to package directions. Do not overcook — its texture should be slightly firm. Keep pasta warm.

In a heavy-gauge saucepan, heat cream, ricotta and Romano cheeses, basil, chives, salt, pepper and garlic, stirring occasionally.

In a separate saucepan, warm tomatoes.

Place pasta on two serving plates. Top with drained scallops, spoon white sauce over and place diced tomatoes on top of white sauce. Serves two.

CALLUAUD'S

2619 McKinney Dallas, TX 75204 (214) 823-5380

Guy Calluaud, owner and chef of Calluaud's restaurant and catering service, was born into a family of chefs. The Calluaud name is famous in France and Morocco, and when Guy and his wife Martine immigrated to the United States in 1974, they decided to carry on the tradition of fine French cuisine in their Dallas restaurant. *Owners:* Guy and Martine Calluaud. Reservations recommended. Closed Sundays.

FRESH SALMON
with CAVIAR SABAYON

1 8-oz. slice of fresh salmon	Juice of ½ lime
½ oz. dry white wine	1 egg yolk
½ teaspoon shallots, chopped	1 teaspoon black American
½ teaspoon unsalted butter	caviar
1 tablespoon heavy cream	Salt and pepper to taste

PREPARATION TIME: 15 MINUTES   COOKING TIME: 15 MINUTES

➤ In a small skillet, combine butter, shallots and white wine.
➤ Season the salmon with salt and pepper to taste. Place the salmon in the skillet and place the skillet over high heat.
➤ When the wine begins to boil, cover the skillet and lower the heat for 1 minute. Then turn the heat off, leaving the skillet covered for 6 minutes.
➤ Remove salmon and place it on a serving dish.
➤ Combine remaining ingredients and heated wine mixture in a small stainless steel bowl. Stir well, and add more salt and pepper if desired.
➤ Place the bowl on a double boiler and stir the mixture as it heats. When thickened, pour the mixture over the salmon and serve. Serves one.

12 South Douglas Avenue Margate, NJ 08402 (609) 822-6100

The Captain's Galley, a 10-minute drive from Atlantic City, has its own retail fish market, the Margate Fisheries, adjacent to the restaurant. The fish market supplies the restaurant with fresh fish every day. The menu changes daily, according to the fish available. Patrons are invited to bring their own wine or beer.
Owner: Harold Coren. Reservations recommended. Open seven days.

FLUKE DAUFAUSKIE

2 lb. fluke (or other flounder) fillets	¼ tablespoon garlic salt
1 onion, chopped	3 dashes Tabasco sauce
¼ lb. mushrooms, diced	2 oz. dry vermouth
⅔ cup mayonnaise	Paprika to taste
⅓ cup prepared mayonnaise	Salt and pepper to taste

PREPARATION TIME: 20 MINUTES   COOKING TIME: 10 MINUTES

▶ Place fillets in a lightly greased baking pan and bake at 350° F. for 15 minutes.

▶ While fillets are baking, sauté onions and mushrooms together.

▶ In a separate bowl, combine mayonnaise, mustard, garlic salt, Tabasco sauce, vermouth, salt and pepper. Blend thoroughly.

▶ Place sautéed onions and mushrooms on cooked fillets and pour sauce over them. Sprinkle with paprika. Bake until browned. Serves four.

860 Second Avenue New York, NY 10017 (212) 697-9538

One of the finest seafood restaurants in New York City, the Captain's Table offers outstanding fish and shellfish dishes, from classic American New England clam chowder to European-style delicacies. The restaurant also features an extensive wine list.
Owner: Gino Musso. Reservations suggested. Closed Sundays.

POACHED STRIPED BASS

3 lb. striped bass fillets, or one small whole striped bass	2 celery stalks, julienned
	¼ onion, julienned
About 3 quarts water, or enough to cover fish in large saucepan	10 parsley sprigs
	3 bay leaves
	10 peppercorns
¼ cup vinegar	Pinch of salt
1 carrot, julienned	

PREPARATION TIME: 10 MINUTES   COOKING TIME: 7 to 8 MINUTES if fillets, 15 to 18 MINUTES if whole fish

▶ Bring water and vinegar to a boil in large saucepan. Add all ingredients except fish and salt, and bring to a boil again.

▶ Add salt. Add fish. Cook for 7 to 8 minutes if fillets, or 15 to 18 minutes if whole fish.

▶ Drain off water. Serve immediately with lemon or light sauce such as Hollandaise sauce. Serves two.

132 West 43rd Street New York, NY 10036 (212) 398-1988

The Century Cafe, located in New York's Times Square area, features an art deco/new wave interior, right down to the neon Loews theatre sign over the bar. Its eclectic menu and lively atmosphere attracts large crowds of businessmen as well as theatre-goers and actors from the surrounding Broadway theatres. The restaurant features art shows and photography exhibits, and varies its menu periodically.

Owner: Phil Scotti. Reservations suggested. Closed Sundays.

BAKED RED SNAPPER

3 lb. fillets of red snapper	¼ teaspoon salt
½ cup orange juice	½ teaspoon pepper
¼ cup Pernod	¼ lb. butter, diced
½ lb. leek, julienned	Orange slices (for garnish)
½ lb. celery, julienned	

PREPARATION TIME: 15 MINUTES   COOKING TIME: 8 MINUTES

▶ Place fish on a baking sheet with a lip, skin side down. Pour orange juice over fish. Add Pernod, salt and pepper, and vegetables. Cover with diced butter and bake at 450° F. for 8 minutes. Serves six.

East 7th Avenue and 22nd Street Tampa, FL 33605 (813) 248-4961

The Columbia Restaurant was founded in 1905 by Casimiro Hernandez, Sr., and since then it has remained under family ownership. It began as a cafe and dining rooms were added gradually through the years. Today, its 11 dining rooms can accommodate 1,660 people simultaneously. The original cafe section is decorated as it was at the turn of the century. The Columbia features Spanish-style food and decor.

Owner: Cesar Gonzmart. Reservations required. Open seven days.

POMPANO PAPILLOTE

8 small fillets (approximately 1 lb. of pompano)	1 teaspoon salt
	Dash of Tabasco sauce
1 stick butter	3 tablespoons dry white wine
1 onion, finely chopped	½ lb. small shrimp, boiled
½ cup flour	½ lb. crab meat
2 cups milk	4 squares of parchment paper
2 egg yolks	10″ × 10″ each)
⅛ teaspoon nutmeg	

PREPARATION TIME: 20 MINUTES   COOKING TIME: 30 MINUTES

▶ Melt butter in a 2-quart saucepan. When foam subsides, add onion and sauté on medium heat for 5 minutes.

▶ Add flour to heated butter and stir well with a wooden spoon until the mixture bubbles. Add milk, nutmeg, salt and Tabasco sauce, stirring constantly to prevent lumps. When thoroughly blended, remove mixture from heat.

▶ In a separate bowl, beat egg yolks lightly. Stir a small amount of the hot mixture in the yolks. Add yolks to heated sauce in saucepan. Mix well and fold in shrimps, crab meat and wine. Cook over medium heat for approximately 2 minutes. Cover and set aside.

▶ Butter parchment paper. Place two heaping tablespoons of the heated mixture in the center of the parchment paper. Place one fillet on top of the mixture, add 2 more heaping tablespoons of mixture, one more fillet, and cover with mixture.

▶ Fold paper over fillet and dressing, crimping edges tightly. Brush melted butter over paper. Bake at 350° F. for 30 minutes. To serve, use a sharp knife to cut the top layer of paper along its crimped edge. Fold back and tuck under bottom layer of paper. Never remove paper. Serves four.

1081 Third Avenue New York, NY 10021 (212) 838-7570

Fiorella specializes in Italian food served in elegant surroundings. Chamber music is featured during Sunday brunch hours.
Owner: Shelly Fireman. Reservations recommended. Open seven days.

FETTUCINE with
FRUTTI di MARE SAUCE

5 oz. olive oil	1 oz. Italian plum tomatoes,
4 cloves garlic, chopped	peeled
½ teaspoon salt	6 oz. sea scallops
¼ teaspoon pepper	6 oz. shrimp
¼ teaspoon basil	6 oz. squid, sliced
1 teaspoon parsley, chopped	1 lb. fettucine
1 teaspoon oregano	

PREPARATION TIME: 20 MINUTES

Boil the fettucine with a pinch of salt for 1 minute or *al dente,* to your taste. Drain and keep warm.

In a skillet, heat 3 oz. olive oil and 3 cloves chopped garlic and sauté until brown.

In a separate pot, crush tomatoes. Add browned garlic, salt, pepper, basil, parsley and oregano, and cook over medium heat for 20 minutes.

Heat remaining 2 oz. olive oil in a skillet and braise scallops, shrimp, mussels, squid and remaining clove of garlic for 3 minutes.

Combine seafood and tomato sauce. Mix with fettucine and serve. Serves four.

The Fish Market

18th & Sansom Streets Philadelphia, PA 19103 (215) 567-3559

The Fish Market has been serving homemade gourmet seafood since 1974. It is located in Center City, Philadelphia.
Owner: Melvyn Siegel. Reservations recommended. Open seven days.

CRAB QUICHE

STEP ONE

1⅓ cups flour	1 egg yolk
½ teaspoon salt	2 to 3 tablespoons cold white
¼ lb. sweet butter	wine

PREPARATION TIME: 15 MINUTES (plus chilling time)

▶ Sift flour and salt together. Add butter in small slices and blend. Add egg yolk and wine to bind ingredients together and form dough. Roll dough flat and fit into a 10-inch or 11-inch quiche or pie pan. Prick bottom of shell with a fork and chill during Step Two.

STEP TWO

1 lb. crab meat	3 egg yolks
6 tablespoons sweet butter	2 cups heavy cream
3 tablespoons parsley, chopped	Dash of nutmeg
1 teaspoon tarragon	4 oz. Jarlsberg cheese, grated
Salt and pepper to taste	Several drops Worcestershire
3 eggs	sauce

PREPARATION TIME: 15 MINUTES   COOKING TIME: 40 to 45 MINUTES

▶ In a large saucepan, sauté crab meat in butter. Add parsley, tarragon, salt and pepper.
▶ In a separate bowl, beat eggs and egg yolks together. Blend in cream, nutmeg, cheese and Worcestershire sauce.
▶ Add crab meat and butter mixture to egg mixture. Mix thoroughly and pour into the chilled shell.
▶ Bake at 450° F. for 10 minutes. Reduce heat to 350° F. and continue baking 30 to 35 minutes or until quiche is golden brown and puffy. Makes one 10-inch or 11-inch quiche.

Galatoire's Restaurant

209 Bourbon Street New Orleans, LA 70130 (504) 525-2021

Galatoire's, a family-run restaurant founded in 1905, is a New Orleans tradition. Little has changed since the restaurant opened nearly 80 years ago—Galatoire's six-page menu lists an unchanging assortment of appetizers and entrées that its regular customers order again and again. Its interior is still reminiscent of the turn of the century, with mirrored walls, tile floor, bentwood chairs and brass trimmings. Galatoire's prides itself on its staff of eight cooks, each of whom can prepare any of the restaurant's dishes. Galatoire's patrons patiently endure the long lines that frequently result from the restaurant's first-come, first-served policy.
Owners: David Gooch, Leon Galatoire, Justin Galatoire Frey. Reservations not accepted. Closed Mondays.

TROUT MEUNIÈRE AMANDINE

4 6-oz. to 8-oz. fillets speckled trout	4 oz. almonds, sliced and toasted
2 cups milk	Juice of 1 lemon
2 cups flour	½ tablespoon parsley, chopped
½ lb. butter	Salt and pepper to taste

PREPARATION TIME: 20 MINUTES

➧ Season fillets with salt and pepper. Dip in milk, then roll in flour.
➧ Fry fillets in hot oil in a shallow pan until golden brown. Place on serving dish.
➧ In a separate pan, melt and continuously whip butter until brown and frothy. Add sliced almonds and lemon juice.
➧ Pour butter sauce over trout. Garnish with chopped parsley. Serves four.

continued

GODCHAUX SALAD

1 head iceberg lettuce, cubed	5 oz. salad oil
2 large tomatoes, cubed	5 oz. red wine vinegar
1 lb. backfin lump crab meat	4 oz. creole mustard
30–35 large shrimp, boiled	2 hard-boiled eggs, sliced
and peeled	8 anchovies

PREPARATION TIME: 15 MINUTES

▶ In a large bowl, combine lettuce, tomatoes, crab meat and shrimp.

▶ In a small bowl, combine salad oil, vinegar and mustard. Mix well.

▶ Pour dressing over salad and toss. Divide salad onto four chilled serving plates and garnish each with ½ hard-boiled egg and two anchovies. Serves four.

OYSTERS en BROCHETTE

24 raw oysters	Flour (to dip skewers in)
12 strips of bacon, cut in half	Salt and pepper to taste
lengthwise	Oil for deep frying
4 8-inch skewers	Toast points
1 egg	Lemon wedges
¾ cup milk	

PREPARATION TIME: 20 MINUTES

▶ Fry bacon until almost crisp.

▶ Alternate six oysters and six half-strips of bacon on each skewer.

▶ In a large bowl, combine egg, milk, salt and pepper. Place flour in a separate bowl.

▶ Dip each skewer in the batter, then roll it in the flour.

▶ Deep fry coated oysters and bacon until golden brown.

▶ Remove from skewers and serve on toast points, garnished with lemon wedges. Serves four as an appetizer or two as a main course.

THE GINGER MAN

51 West 64th Street New York, NY 10023 (212) 399-2358

The Ginger Man, founded in 1964, was originally a 60-seat restaurant that served primarily hamburgers. Today, the 190-seat restaurant specializes in gourmet cafe-style food. Its three owners have restaurants in New York, Coconut Grove, Miami, and Beverly Hills. The Ginger Man takes its name from a play, written by J.P. Donleavy, in which co-owner actor Patrick O'Neal appeared. *Owners:* Michael O'Neal, Patrick O'Neal, Ture Tufresson. Reservations recommended. Open seven days.

POACHED NORWEGIAN SALMON

STEP ONE

1 7-lb. side of Norwegian salmon fillet, skinned	Juice of 1 lemon
	½ teaspoon salt
2 cups dry white wine	

PREPARATION TIME: 10 MINUTES   COOKING TIME: 15 to 20 MINUTES

▶ Place salmon in a large pan deep enough to hold 2 to 3 inches of liquid.

▶ Pour wine, lemon juice and salt over fish. Cover pan with aluminum foil and bake at 325° F. for 15 to 20 minutes, or until fish feels firm to the touch.

▶ Place fish in refrigerator to chill, and carry out Step Two.

STEP TWO

10 new potatoes	1 head romaine lettuce
1 bunch scallions, finely chopped	1 lb. cherry tomatoes
	Black olives (for garnish)
Olive oil (for sautéing)	Anchovies (for garnish)
2 lb. green beans, trimmed	Capers (for garnish)
6 hard-boiled eggs	Lemon-mayonnaise dressing*

▶ Boil potatoes until tender. Allow to cool, and slice each into 3 or 4 pieces. Set aside.

▶ Lightly sauté scallions in olive oil, and pour over potatoes.

▶ Blanch green beans, and put them in refrigerator to chill.

▶ Gently tear lettuce and place an equal amount on each of 6 individual serving plates. Slice salmon and place on lettuce. Arrange potatoes, chilled beans, sliced hard-boiled eggs and cherry tomatoes atop fish. Garnish with black olives, anchovies and capers.

*LEMON-MAYONNAISE DRESSING

3 egg yolks	3 to 4 tablespoons lemon juice
⅓ teaspoon salt	2 tablespoons boiling water
¼ teaspoon white pepper	2 tablespoons dijon mustard
1½ cups olive oil	

PREPARATION TIME: 10 MINUTES

▶ Blend all ingredients thoroughly. Pour over salad. Serves six.

Gladstone's

17300 Pacific Coast Highway Pacific Palisades, CA 90272 (213) GL4-FISH
and
900 Bayside Drive Newport Beach, CA 92660 (714) 645-FISH

Gladstone's 4 Fish's lengthy menu lists a wide variety of fresh fish and shellfish. Both branches, founded in 1971, feature Southern California cuisine. The Pacific Palisades restaurant offers a splendid view of the sea.
Owner: Robert J. Morris. Reservations strongly recommended. Open seven days.

GLADSTONE'S LOBSTER SCAMPI

4 1-lb. or 1½ lb. lobsters	Scampi Butter*

PREPARATION TIME: 10 MINUTES   COOKING TIME: 9 to 10 MINUTES

▶ Boil lobsters for approximately 6 minutes. Cut in half; pull off craws and veins.
▶ Cover with scampi butter. Place under broiler for 3 to 4 minutes. Serves four.

*SCAMPI BUTTER

½ lb. butter	1 cup brandy
½ tablespoon paprika	¼ cup white wine
½ tablespoon flour	⅛ cup scallops, finely chopped
¼ cup garlic, freshly chopped	⅛ cup parsley, fresh chopped

PREPARATION TIME: 25 MINUTES

▶ Place softened butter in bowl. Add all ingredients except brandy, and beat with a wire whip for 10 minutes.* Add brandy, and whip 10 minutes more, scraping butter from sides of bowl.

Use an electric mixer, if you prefer.

1489 Airways Boulevard Memphis, TN 38114 (901) 458-2648

Grisanti's Restaurant, in downtown Memphis, has been a Grisanti family tradition since 1909. The cuisine is predominantly Italian, but seafood and steaks are also featured. Owner John Grisanti has twice held the world's record for the highest price paid for a bottle of wine sold at auction. In both cases, the proceeds of the sales went to the St. Jude's Children's Research Hospital in Memphis.
Owner: John A. Grisanti. Reservations not accepted. Closed Sundays.

This appetizer is not on Grisanti's everyday menu—it is prepared only for special occasions.

SHRIMP in WHITE WINE SAUCE

12 medium- to large-size shrimp	¼ lb. softened butter, cut into chips
½ cup white wine	Lemon wedges
2 small shallots (or green onions), chopped	

PREPARATION TIME: 15 MINUTES

▶ Sauté shrimp and shallots in wine.
▶ Remove shrimp and set aside. Simmer remaining sauce on medium heat until it is reduced to about ¼ cup of liquid.
▶ Remove pan from heat, and slowly stir in presoftened butter chips, one at a time.
▶ Pour through a small strainer to remove the shallots.
▶ Place three shrimp on each of four small serving dishes. Pour sauce over them and garnish with lemon wedges. Serves four.

Hungry Tiger Inc.
RESTAURANT & SEAFOOD OYSTER BAR

31 locations in Westchester, Palos Verdes, Hollywood and Palm Springs, California, and in Arizona, Nevada and Texas.

The Hungry Tiger seafood restaurants prefer to be known as a "non-chain chain." Each individual restaurant is decorated to suit its location, and each features a blackboard that lists regional specialities in addition to the chef's special creations. The printed menu is the same in each restaurant. The original Hungry Tiger restaurant was opened in 1962 by Bob Prescott, a member of the World War II squadron known as the Flying Tigers. Prescott founded Flying Tiger Airlines and eventually began flying in live Maine lobsters to his restaurant every day. Today, more than 10,000 pounds of Maine lobster is distributed to Hungry Tiger restaurants every month.

HUNGRY TIGER CLAM CHOWDER

2 oz. butter	Salt and white pepper to taste
1 cup onion, diced	1 small bay leaf
1 cup leek, white part only, diced	½ teaspoon thyme
⅓ cup green pepper, diced	⅔ cup raw potato, diced
2 tablespoons flour	2 oz. dry white wine
1 pint water and 1 pint clam juice *or* 1 quart fish stock	1 cup chopped clams, drained
	½ cup warm half-and-half

PREPARATION TIME: 20 MINUTES   COOKING TIME: 35 MINUTES

🐟 Melt butter in a saucepan. Add onion, leek, celery and green pepper and cook until tender but not browned.
🐟 Stir flour into butter mixture and cook over very low heat for 2 to 3 minutes. Add water and clam juice or fish stock, salt and pepper, bay leaf and thyme.
🐟 Bring mixture to a boil and add potato and wine. Cover and simmer 30 minutes or until the potatoes are soft.
🐟 Add clams and simmer 5 minutes more. Remove the bay leaf and stir in warm cream just before serving. Serves six.

JANICE'S
FISH PLACE

570 Hudson Street New York, NY 10014 (212) 243-4212

Located on the west side of New York's Greenwich Village, Janice's Fish Place features a blend of Eastern and Western cuisines. Seafood entrées are accompanied by bowls of brown rice, soy nuggets, sunflower seeds and raisins, and many dishes are complemented by snowpeas and red szechuan peppercorns. The restaurant has a wood-and-brick dining room and a glass-enclosed sidewalk cafe that provides diners with a view of one of New York City's oldest neighborhoods.

Owner: Janice Reuben. Reservations suggested. Open seven days.

BLUEFISH MISO

STEP ONE

2 bluefish steaks (approximately 12 oz. each)	4 tablespoons cooking wine
4 tablespoons butter	2 tablespoons lemon juice
	Salt and pepper to taste

PREPARATION TIME: 10 MINUTES   COOKING TIME: 13 MINUTES

🐟 Place steaks in a buttered baking pan and broil for 2 to 3 minutes.

🐟 Heat oven to 250° F. and transfer fish from broiler oven. Bake for 10 minutes.

🐟 While fish bakes, sauté mushrooms in butter. Blend in cooking wine, lemon juice, salt and pepper.

STEP TWO

2 teaspoons miso paste	2 teaspoons brandy
1 teaspoon fresh ginger, chopped	2 teaspoons soya sauce
2 oz. cooking wine	Paprika (for garnish)
	Parsley (for garnish)

PREPARATION TIME: 10 MINUTES

🐟 Combine all ingredients except paprika and parsley together in a bowl to form a sauce.

🐟 When fish is baked, transfer it to a platter. Place mushrooms in butter mixture on top of the steaks. Pour sauce over steaks and mushrooms. Garnish with paprika and parsley. Serves two.

172

LEGAL SEA FOODS®

"If it isn't fresh, it isn't Legal."SM

Four branches in Massachusetts—2 in Boston, 1 in Cambridge, and 1 in Chestnut Hill.

All four Massachusetts locations of Legal Sea Foods serve fresh seafood in a no-frills fashion. The food can be taken out or eaten in the restaurant, although tables are sometimes scarce because of Legal Sea Foods's first-come, first-served policy. Legal Sea Foods has been serving its fish and shellfish dishes since 1967.
Owner: George Berkowitz. Reservations not accepted. Open seven days.

MUSSELS au GRATIN

⅓ bottle French blanc de blanc	5 lbs. fresh mussels, cleaned (shells scrubbed)
½ cup melted butter	½ bunch parsley, chopped
8 cloves garlic, finely chopped	2 cups crackers, crushed
1 tablespoon salt	1 cup mild cheddar cheese, grated
1 tablespoon pepper	Parsley for garnish
½ cup onions, chopped	Lemon wedges for garnish

PREPARATION TIME: 20 MINUTES   COOKING TIME: 10 MINUTES

▶ In a 6-quart pot, combine wine, ¼ cup melted butter, 4 cloves garlic, salt, pepper and onions. Bring mixture to a boil, then reduce temperature to medium heat and add mussels.

▶ Steam mussels in broth until they open (approximately 8 minutes), then remove them from the broth. Break off top shells, and place remaining shells and meat on a baking sheet.

▶ Mix 4 cloves of garlic with parsley and knead into the semihard butter. Spoon a generous amount of this garlic butter over each mussel.

▶ Bake mussels at 450° F. for 5 minutes. While they're baking, combine crushed crackers, ¼ cup chopped onions and ¼ cup melted butter.

▶ Remove mussels from oven and sprinkle with cheddar cheese, making sure to cover all the mussels. Add the crumb topping over the cheese.

▶ Return mussels to oven for an additional 6 minutes or until cracker crumbs are brown.

▶ Garnish with parsley and lemon wedges. Serves four to six.

LOCKE-OBER CAFÉ
EST·1875

3 and 4 Winter Place Boston, MA 02108 (617) 542-1340

Locke-Ober, established in 1875, derives its hyphenated name not from a partnership but a rivalry. Frank Locke and Louis Ober each ran a restaurant in the Boston alley called Winter Place. Locke and Ober competed for customers in the late 19th century. Following their deaths the restaurant known as Locke-Ober was formally created in 1901 by Emil Camus, who synthesized the two restaurants and called the establishment Locke-Ober. The restaurant specializes in cuisine that blends the cooking styles of Locke and Ober—Ober favored French cuisine and vintage wines, Locke preferred Maine lobsters, steaks and hard liquor. Locke-Ober has several dining rooms, both public and private.
Owner: David Ray. Reservations suggested. Closed Sundays.

LOBSTER and SHRIMP AMERICAINE

½ lb. fresh lobster meat, cut in large dice	6 tablespoons sherry
1 lb. raw shrimp, shelled	Parsley, chopped
1 1-lb. can tomatoes, finely chopped (reserve liquid)	2 tablespoons mirepoix*

PREPARATION TIME: 10 MINUTES   COOKING TIME: 10 MINUTES

➤ Place mirepoix*, lobster and shrimp in sauté pan and heat.
➤ Add tomatoes, sherry and parsley to the mixture, along with ½ the reserved tomato liquid. Simmer gently for 10 minutes.
➤ Serve very hot on crisp toast. Serves two.

*MIREPOIX

This flavoring mixture for soups, stews and sauces was reportedly named after a French duke who lived during the reign of Louis XV.

½ small carrot, finely chopped	Pinch of thyme, pounded fine
1 small onion, finely chopped	1 bay leaf, pounded fine
½ stalk of celery, finely chopped	2 tablespoons butter (more if needed)

PREPARATION TIME: 10 MINUTES

➤ Place all ingredients in a saucepan and stew over low heat until tender. If necessary, add more butter to prevent burning.

LONDON CHOP HOUSE

and Gourmet Shelf

155 West Congress Detroit, MI 48226 (313) 962-1087

The London Chop House, in downtown Detroit, was founded in 1938. It features a Continental/American menu and an extensive wine list. Sometimes called "the 21 Club of the Midwest," the Chop House offers both seafood and meat dishes and provides entertainment nightly.

Owner: Max J. Pincus. Reservations recommended. Closed Sundays.

PÂTÉ de POISSON

1 lb. scallops, cleaned	¼ teaspoon white pepper
12 oysters, shucked	½ bunch mint, chopped
2 oz. salmon caviar	1 bunch basil, chopped
1 4-oz. salmon fillet	8 oz. white wine
2 egg whites	8 oz. white wine vinegar
4 tablespoons sweet butter	4 oz. shallots, coarsely chopped
10 oz. whipping cream	1 oz. white peppercorns
1¼ teaspoons whipping cream	12 tablespoons sweet butter

PREPARATION TIME: 30 MINUTES   COOKING TIME: 6 MINUTES

▶ Puree the scallops together with egg whites until smooth. Set aside and chill.

▶ In an electric mixer, whip butter and white pepper until smooth. Gradually fold in scallop puree while whipping on high speed. Blend well.

▶ Turn mixer to low speed and slowly add whipping cream. When all the cream is added, blend thoroughly. Remove from mixer, and gently fold in mint and half the basil. Then fold in oysters and caviar.

▶ Place half the pâté mixture in a buttered terrine dish, preferably one that's approximately 4½ inches deep and 6 inches long. Position the salmon fillet in the center, and cover with remaining pâté. Smooth the top of the pâté.

▶ Place buttered parchment directly on the surface of the pâté, and cover parchment with foil. Bake in a water bath at 325° F.for approximately 1 hour.

▶ While the pâté bakes, combine white wine, white wine vinegar, shallots and peppercorns in an acid-resistant pot. Reduce liquid over high heat until nearly none is left. Strain and reserve liquid.

▶ When the pâté is nearly done, bring the strained liquid to a rapid boil. Gradually whisk in butter. Season with salt and pepper. Remove from heat and transfer to a stainless steel bowl. Whisk for a few seconds. Blend in remaining basil.

▶ Pour sauce on serving plate. Slice the pâté and place on top of the sauce. Serves six.

Maile Restaurant

Kahala Hilton Hotel 5000 Kahala Avenue Honolulu, HI 96816 (808) 734-2211

The Maile Restaurant takes its name from the maile leaf, once worn only by Hawaiian chiefs. Today the leaf is woven into leis and worn on special occasions to signify royal service and treatment. In a state noted for luaus and casual eating, the Maile offers gracious dining in an orchid-filled room. The menu is a mixture of international cuisine and Hawaiian specialties.
Chef: Andreas Knapp. Reservations suggested. Open seven days.

MAHI MAHI CAPRICE

The dolphin fish (not the mammal) is called mahi mahi in Hawaii.

2 7-oz. mahi mahi fillets	2 tablespoons whipped cream
3 oz. sweet butter	(no sugar)
1 cup dry white wine	Salt and pepper to taste
2 medium shallots, finely	Buttered wax paper
chopped	Garnish (optional)
4 oz. creamed mushrooms	6 oz. Parisienne potatoes
½ banana, cut lengthwise	2 spears broccoli
	2 sprigs parsley

PREPARATION TIME: 15 MINUTES   COOKING TIME: 5 MINUTES

🐟 Season fillets with salt and pepper. In a skillet, brown both sides of each fillet in hot butter for 1 minute. Add wine and shallots. Cover with buttered wax paper and simmer in the oven at 420° F. for 5 to 6 minutes.

🐟 Remove fish. Transfer liquid to saucepan and heat on high until reduced by half. Add creamed mushrooms and bring to fast boil. Remove from heat and stir in whipped cream.

🐟 Place fish on serving dish and top with mushroom sauce and sliced banana. Place under broiler until sauce is golden brown.

🐟 Garnish, if you prefer. Serves two.

Mama's
of san francisco

1177 California Street San Francisco, CA 94108 (415) 928-0952

Mama's opened in 1951 as an ice-cream parlor featuring sherbets, sandwiches and hamburgers. In those days, patrons had to wait on long lines for space at one of Mama's tables. Today it has three California locations, two featuring modified cafeteria-style service, the other, on Nob Hill, featuring full service and an extensive, eclectic menu from breakfast through dessert. The decor is pure California, with latticework gazebos, tile floors, porcelain-topped tables and an abundance of light and flowers.
Owners: Frances (Mama) Sanchez and Michael (Papa) Sanchez. Reservations suggested for dinner. Open seven days.

FRESH PETRALE
with MADIERA SAUCE

4 petrale fillets	4 teaspoons butter
Flour (for dusting fish)	4 teaspoons lemon juice
4 eggs	4 teaspoons Madeira wine
¼ cup olive oil	Pinch of flour

PREPARATION TIME: 20 MINUTES

▶ Dust fillets lightly with flour.
▶ Heat olive oil in a saucepan on medium heat.
▶ Beat the eggs lightly with a wire whisk. Dip the fillets into the egg mixture.
▶ Place fish in heated olive oil and brown lightly on each side. When brown, transfer to a serving dish.
▶ Pour oil out of saucepan and wipe pan quickly.
▶ Into the warm pan add butter, lemon juice, Madeira and flour. Add parsley, salt, and pepper to taste. Spoon over petrale and serve. Serves four.

8368 Melrose Avenue Los Angeles, CA 90069 (213) 655-1991

Ma Maison, founded in 1973, is located on the border of Beverly Hills. This renowned Hollwood gathering place serves French bistro style cuisine and, according to owner Patrick Terrail, seafood is an increasingly popular item.

Owner: Patrick Terrail. Reservations recommended. Closed Sundays.

MARINATED SALMON
with TOMATO and MINT

1 tomato, peeled and seeded	Salt and pepper to taste
3 tablespoons olive oil	6–8 oz. salmon fillet
10 mint leaves, cut into fine	Juice of ½ lemon
chiffonade, or julienned	Juice of ½ lime
2 shallots, finely minced	

PREPARATION TIME: 20 MINUTES

▶ To prepare sauce, in a bowl, combine tomato, olive oil, mint, shallots, salt, and pepper, and let marinate.

▶ Cut salmon lengthwise into very thin slices. Combine lime juice, lemon juice, olive oil, salt, and pepper and spoon over fish. Let stand 3 to 5 minutes.

▶ To serve, spoon sauce onto plate. Arrange salmon on sauce and garnish with mint sprig and slice of lime. Serves two as appetizers.

the
MARYLAND
CRAB HOUSE

237 Third Avenue New York, NY 10003 (212) 598-4890

The Maryland Crab House, formerly known as Cincinnati, is New York's first authentic crab house. Crabs are delivered to the restaurant every day, enabling it to feature a variety of freshly prepared crab dishes that are usually difficult to find in New York. In addition, the Crab House serves fresh fish in season, shellfish, seafood salads and some non-seafood items.
Owner: Andrew Silverman. Reservations not accepted. Open seven days.

JUMBO MARYLAND CRAB CAKES

2 lb. backfin lump crab meat	2 teaspoons Worcestershire
1 egg, beaten	sauce
2 slices white bread with	Juice of 1 lemon
crusts removed, cubed	Old Bay seasoning to taste
¾ cup mayonnaise	Tabasco sauce to taste
1 tablespoon mustard	Salt to taste
	Oil for frying

PREPARATION TIME: 15 MINUTES   COOKING TIME: 8 to 10 MINUTES

▶ Remove cartilage from crab meat.
▶ In a large bowl, add all ingredients and fold gently but thoroughly. Season to taste.
▶ Shape ingredients into 12 6-oz. cakes.
▶ Coat a large frying pan with just enough oil to keep the cakes from sticking. Cook cakes until golden brown, about 4 minutes on each side. Serves six.

NEW DEAL

152 Spring Street New York, NY 10012 (212) 431-3663

The New Deal features art deco surroundings and murals depicting the New Deal era. A jazz piano and bass add to the atmosphere, which is reminiscent of New York's old Cotton Club. The restaurant prides itself on serving fresh food with "simplicity and creativity." *Owner:* Harvey Riezenman. Reservations suggested on weekends. Closed Mondays.

SOLE PISTOU

4 6-oz. fish fillets	4 oz. white wine
¾ cup flour	16 oz. cream
1 egg, lightly beaten	1½ teaspoons garlic, chopped
1 cup fresh breadcrumbs	20 fresh basil leaves
3 to 4 oz. clarified butter	Salt and pepper
16 oz. fish stock	

PREPARATION TIME: 20 MINUTES

Dust fish lightly on both sides with flour, then dip *one side of each fillet only* in egg and breadcrumbs.

Sauté fillets in clarified butter over medium flame until they're slightly crisp and have a golden crust. Turn fillets to cook both sides.

In a separate pan, reduce stock and wine over medium heat until the mixture is almost a glaze. Add cream, and reduce by half.

Add garlic and basil to reduced sauce and simmer over low heat for 5 minutes. Season to taste.

Ladle sauce, with basil leaves, onto serving plate. Place fish carefully atop the sauce. Serves four.

NODELDINI'S

1311 Madison Avenue New York, NY 10028 (212) 369-5677

Nodeldini's is one of five seafood restaurants owned and operated by four New York businessmen. Each has the same menu, featuring a wide assortment of fresh seafood as well as beef dishes. The first restaurant in the chain, Hobeau's, was founded in 1967; Nodeldini's opened in 1973.

Owners: Robert Bernadini, Richard Knodel, Joseph M. Adinaro, Paul Schylinski. Although reservations are not taken, the restaurant tends to be crowded and the owners suggest that you call ahead. Open seven days.

SEAFOOD KABOBS

12 individual sea scallops, ¾ lb.	2 green peppers
12 medium size shrimp, peeled and deveined, about ¾ lb.	4 small mushroom caps
1 large white onion	¼ lb. butter
2 red peppers	1 tablespoon freshly crushed garlic
	2 servings of rice

PREPARATION TIME: 15 MINUTES   COOKING TIME: 20 to 25 MINUTES

► Prepare rice according to package directions.

► Cut the onion and peppers into 2-inch squares.

► Using either metal skewers or thin wooden ones alternating the above ingredients (except the mushroom caps), start with a slice of onion, then a scallop, pepper, shrimp, etc. End each kabob with a mushroom cap.

► Melt butter with garlic, do not burn.

► Arrange the skewers on a broiling pan. Evenly pour half the butter and garlic mixture over the kabobs.

► Broil the kabobs for 10-15 minutes, turn the kabobs, pour the rest of the butter and garlic over them, and broil for another 10 minutes.

Serve on a bed of rice. Serves two.

Dulaney Valley Road Phoenix, MD 21131 (301) 252-3100

Peerce's Plantation, established in 1941, is located on the site where a country store owned by William E. Peerce originally stood. Peerce decided to build a restaurant on the land, and was joined in his venture by Duff and Marie Lake, whose son is the current owner of the restaurant. Peerce's Plantation offers a wide range of foods, and is noted for its Irish coffee and mint juleps.

Owner: Peerce Lake. Reservations suggested. Open seven days.

OYSTERS CASINO

24 oysters in shells	1 teaspoon paprika
6 slices bacon	¼ teaspoon white pepper,
1 medium onion, sliced	ground
½ green pepper, minced	2 to 3 dashes seafood
2 tablespoons chives, chopped	seasoning
2 tablespoons Parmesan	
cheese, grated	

PREPARATION TIME: 15 MINUTES   COOKING TIME: 7 to 8 MINUTES

▶ Open shells, leave oyster meat in bottom and discard top shell.
▶ In a medium fry pan, sauté bacon until crisp. Remove bacon, crumble and reserve. Pour off excess fat, add onion and pepper, and sauté for 5 minutes.
▶ In a small bowl, mix chives, cheese, paprika, pepper and seafood seasoning. Blend into sautéed vegetables. Add reserved bacon.
▶ Arrange oysters on shallow baking pan. Spoon 1 teaspoon of bacon mixture on each opened oyster. Bake at 400° F. for 7 to 8 minutes. Makes 24 appetizers.

Peerce's Plantation's Executive Chef Josef Gohring suggests you serve oysters casino with melted butter.

182

𝔓ort 𝔖t. 𝔏ouis

R E S T A U R A N T

15 North Central Avenue Clayton, MO 63105 (314) 727-1142

The owners of Port St. Louis are proud of the fact that, despite their distance from the sea, they do not serve any frozen seafood. Co-owner Wade DeWoskin orders small amounts of fresh fish and shellfish from several East coast suppliers, knowing that if his order leaves the East coast at 11 a.m., he can expect delivery in time for dinner. Port St. Louis has been providing freshly prepared seafood for its customers since 1959.

Owners: Wade and Lois DeWoskin. Reservations suggested. Open seven days.

LEMON SOLE BIRDS

½ cup green onions, chopped	10 or 12 small fillets of lemon
½ cup celery, chopped	sole
2 cloves garlic, minced	3 tablespoons melted butter
4 tablespoons butter	Salt and pepper to taste
1 cup cooked shrimp, cut in	Parmesan cheese, grated (to
small pieces	sprinkle on fillets)
1 cup crab meat (not canned;	Paprika (to sprinkle on fillets)
preferably king crab legs)	1 lemon, sliced
⅔ cup bread crumbs	

PREPARATION TIME: 15 MINUTES   COOKING TIME: 8–10 MINUTES

▶ Sauté onions, celery and garlic in 4 tablespoons butter until vegetables are soft. Gently fold in shrimp, crab meat, parsley, salt and pepper, being careful not to break up crab meat. Add bread crumbs.

▶ Place a large spoonful of the stuffing mixture in the center of each sole fillet, and fold fillet up around it.

▶ Brush tops of fillets with melted butter and sprinkle with Parmesan cheese and paprika. Bake at 350° F. for 8 to 10 minutes or until nicely browned. Garnish with lemon slices. Serves six.

S. & D. OYSTER COMPANY

2701 McKinney Avenue Dallas, TX 75204 (214) 823-6350

The S & D Oyster Company, just a few minutes from downtown Dallas, is located in a 100-year-old building that used to be a grocery store. This unpretentious restaurant, with painted brick walls and cement floors, offers an assortment of well-prepared seafood dishes from appetizers to entrées.

Owner: Herbert B. Story. Reservations not accepted. Closed Sunday.

SPICY SHRIMP DIP

2 lb peeled, deveined shrimp	1 small onion, grated
8 oz. package cream cheese	4 teaspoons Tabasco sauce
½ cup mayonnaise	1 tablespoon Lawry's seasoned
1 cup thousand island salad	salt
dressing	1 tablespoon fresh ground
¼ cup minced fresh green	horseradish
onions	

PREPARATION TIME: 15 MINUTES

▶ Boil shrimp. Chop cooked shrimp.

▶ Blend softened cream cheese with mayonnaise and salad dressing.

▶ Stir in shrimp, minced onions, grated onion, Tabasco sauce, seasoned salt, and horseradish.

▶ Serve with crackers or raw vegetables. Makes about 1½ quarts.

BROILED FISH

Broiled fish is particularly popular at S & D. Lighter than fried fish, it's a good warm weather entrée. This simple recipe takes 20 minutes to prepare, and can be eaten plain or with your choice of seafood sauces.

2 lb. fresh fish fillets	¼ cup butter
(red snapper, speckled trout	Paprika
and flounder are suggested)	1 lemon, sliced
1 teaspoon lemon juice	Parsley

PREPARATION TIME: 10 MINUTES   COOKING TIME: 10–15 MINUTES

▶ Place fish in oven-proof dish.

▶ Melt butter in saucepan. Add lemon juice to melted butter.

▶ Pour lemon butter over fish. Splash a few drops of water on top of it. Sprinkle with paprika.

▶ Broil for 10-15 minutes, depending on thickness of fish. The fish is done when it flakes easily with a fork and its color is milky white instead of translucent.

▶ Garnish with lemon slices and parsley. Serves six.

Star ᵒ͓ₜₕₑ Sea Room

1360 North Harbor Drive San Diego, CA 92101 (619) 232-7408

The Star of The Sea Room is one of a chain of California restaurants owned and managed by Anthony's Fish Grottos. The company's first restaurant, called Anthony's Fish Grotto, was established in 1946 by Catherine Ghio. Her sons Tod and Anthony and son-in-law Roy Weber eventually joined her in overseeing the expanding chain of fine seafood restaurants. The Star of the Sea Room offers a magnificent view of the San Diego harbor in addition to a wide range of freshly prepared seafoods. Mrs. Ghio, now in her eighties, still oversees the restaurant's kitchens.

Owners: The Ghio and Weber families. Reservations required. Open seven days.

CHARCOAL-BROILED SWORDFISH

STEP ONE	
1½ cups olive oil	3 cloves or garlic, crushed

PREPARATION TIME: Overnight

▶ Add crushed garlic to olive oil and allow to marinate overnight. This creates the garlic oil needed in Step Two.

STEP TWO	1 teaspoon monosodium
1¼ cups garlic oil	glutamate
2 cups ketchup	Juice of ½ lemon
¼ cup Worcestershire sauce	2 drops Liquid Smoke
3 tablespoons dry mustard	Pinch of thyme
¾ cup sherry	Salt and pepper to taste

PREPARATION TIME: 5 MINUTES

▶ Place all ingredients in a closed container and shake well. Set aside.

STEP THREE	
4 swordfish steaks, ¾-inch to 1-inch thick, skinned	Bunch of fresh parsley

▶ Marinate fish in sauce from Step Two in a deep dish for 4 to 8 hours, turning 3 or 4 times while marinating.

▶ Place fish over a moderately hot charcoal fire. Reserve marinade.

▶ Turn gently four times. Using the parsley as a basting brush, baste the fish with marinade as it cooks over the coals for 20 minutes.

Alternative Method

▶ Place the fish on a foil-lined broiler pan and broil for 20 minutes, basting as recommended above. Turn fish after 10 minutes.

▶ Serves four.   *continued* 〰▶

STAR of the SEA SALAD
with STAR of INDIA DRESSING

½ cup mayonnaise	1 teaspoon red wine vinegar
¼ cup milk	1 teaspoon red cocktail sauce
2 tablespoons white or golden raisins	3 hearts of romaine lettuce (about 6 cups)
1 tablespoon sugar	8 oz. cooked shrimp, crab or lobster meat
1 teaspoon curry powder	
1 teaspoon lemon juice	

PREPARATION TIME: 10 MINUTES

In a bowl, combine mayonnaise, milk, raisins, sugar, curry powder, lemon juice, red wine vinegar and cocktail sauce. Blend well.

Gently tear the hearts of lettuce and arrange equal amounts on each of 4 serving plates. Arrange seafood over lettuce.

Pour dressing over salad. Serves four.

CLAMS GENOVESE

1 cup cooked fettucine or other flat noodles	½ cup chopped clams
½ cup thick cream sauce, thinned with clam juice	¼ cup grated Parmesan cheese
	Pepper, freshly ground

PREPARATION TIME: 15 MINUTES

In large bowl mix noodles with heated cream sauce, clams and cheese.

Add pepper to taste. Serves two to three, as an appetizer.

Tadich Grill

THE ORIGINAL COLD DAY RESTAURANT

240 California Street San Francisco, CA 94111 (415) 391-2373

The Tadich Grill began in 1849, during the California Gold Rush, as a small but prosperous coffee shop run by three Yugoslavian immigrants. The shop, called The New World Coffee Stand, was frequented by County Assessor Alexander Badlam, Jr. In 1882, Badlam ran for re-election and infuriated his opponents and the voters with his slogan, "It's a cold day when I get left." He was overwhelmingly defeated and sought refuge at the coffee shop, where his opponents dumped a wagonload of ice on the doorstep. The incident was covered in the newspapers and the coffee stand became known as The Cold Day. In 1887 John Tadich, employed by the coffee shop for 16 years, became the owner. An earthquake forced him to relocate, and his former partner also opened a new restaurant, naming his establishment The Cold Day Restaurant. Tadich, believing that he was entitled to use that nickname, named his place Tadich Grill, The Original Cold Day Restaurant. Tom Buich joined Tadich in 1913, and eventually he and his brothers bought the restaurant. Tom's nephews now own the Tadich Grill, which features a wide selection of seafood.

Owners: Steve and Bob Buich. Reservations not accepted. Closed Sundays.

Chef John Canepa suggests that this entree be served with hot buttered noodles and a vegetable side dish.

SCALLOPS SAUTÉ
a la CANEPA

1 tablespoon flour	2 oz. chardonnay or chablis
2 tablespoons olive oil	6 oz. whipping cream
4 oz. butter	½ cup sour cream
3 tablespoons onion, chopped	1 tablespoon chives
Pinch of salt	1 teaspoon parsley, chopped
Pinch of cayenne pepper	Juice of 1 lemon
Pinch of nutmeg	

PREPARATION TIME: 25 MINUTES

▶ Drain scallops. Dust well with flour.
▶ In a sauté skillet, heat oil and 2 oz. butter over medium heat. Add scallops, turning until lightly browned.
▶ Add chopped onion, salt, cayenne pepper and nutmeg; heat, stirring occasionally for 2 minutes.

continued ▶

Add wine and continue heating to reduce wine. Add whipping cream and heat for 4 minutes. Remove from heat.

Stir in sour cream, chives, chopped parsley, 2 oz. solid butter and lemon juice. Serves two.

BAKED AVOCADO and SHRIMP DIAVOLO with RICE

2 ripe avocados	Pinch of salt
2 tablespoons butter	Pinch of pepper
1 tablespoon onion, chopped	Pinch of nutmeg
1 tablespoon green bell pepper, chopped	1 cup shrimp, peeled and boiled
1 tablespoon celery, chopped	½ cup rice
½ teaspoon dry mustard	2 slices Monterey cheese
4 tablespoons whipping cream	4 mushroom cups
2 tablespoons sherry	

PREPARATION TIME: 15 MINUTES   COOKING TIME: 15 MINUTES

Cut each avocado lengthwise. Using a tablespoon, scoop out the pulp and set shells aside. Dice the pulp.

In a saucepan, melt butter. Sauté onion, bell pepper and celery until tender. Remove from heat and transfer ingredients to a bowl.

Add mustard, cream, wine, salt, pepper and nutmeg to ingredients in bowl. Blend well. Add avocado pulp and cooked shrimp. Mix, and place in avocado shells.

Boil rice for 20 minutes. Strain, and put in buttered baking dish. Arrange avocados on top of rice. Top each avocado with ½ slice of cheese and mushroom cup.

Bake at 350° F. for 15 minutes. Serves four.

Chef John Canepa calls this "a simple and tasty preparation."

FILLET of SOLE ALL'AGRO

6 pieces fillet of sole	2 oz. dry white wine
1 tablespoon flour	Juice of 1 lemon
1 egg	1 tablespoon parsley, chopped
Pinch of salt	1 tablespoon butter
Pinch of pepper	1 lemon, sliced
4 tablespoons olive oil	

PREPARATION TIME: 15 MINUTES

Place fillets in a bowl and flour lightly; break an egg into the bowl and add salt and pepper. Mix fillets and ingredients throughly.

Pour olive oil in a large pan and heat to medium temperature. Add one fillet at a time, heat for 4 to 5 minutes on each side.

Remove fillets from heat and place on serving dish. Drain excess olive oil from pan. Add wine and heat for 2 seconds. Stir in lemon juice, chopped parsley and butter. When mixture foams and thickens, pour over fish. Garnish with lemon slices.

RESTAURANT

3172 North Sheridan Road Chicago, IL 60657 (312) 935-0350

Tango, voted one of Chicago's favorite restaurants for six consecutive years in *Chicago Magazine's* annual reader's poll, is devoted exclusively to preparing and serving French-style seafood. The restaurant features three dining areas and knowledgeable, helpful waiters, many of whom joined Tango when it first opened 10 years ago. Tango offers a special discount to early diners who place their order by 5:45 p.m. and finish their meal by 7:00 p.m. *Owner:* George Badonsky. Reservations recommended. Closed Mondays.

BAKED HALIBUT
with ORANGE PECAN SAUCE

8 7-oz halibut fillets	4 shallots, chopped
1 cup dry white wine	½ cup pecans, chopped
1 cup fish stock (fumet)	Juice of 1 lemon
5 oranges	1 bouquet garni*
8 oz. butter	3 tablespoons heavy cream
½ teaspoon cornstarch	Salt and pepper to taste

PREPARATION TIME: 20 MINUTES   COOKING TIME: 10 MINUTES

🐟 Season the fillets with salt and pepper on both sides and place in a buttered baking dish, along with shallots and bouquet garni. Pour wine and fish stock over fillets to moisten them, and bake at 350° F. until the fish flakes when tested with a fork.

🐟 When fish is cooked, strain the liquid and reserve. Cover fish to keep it warm.

🐟 Use a zester to remove the orange peel from the oranges, being careful not to scrape the white fiber beneath the peel. Set strips of peel aside.

🐟 Squeeze the oranges and mix their juice with the liquid from the cooked fish. Add lemon juice, and cook in a skillet over medium heat until the liquid is reduced by one third. Add cream and cornstarch, diluted with a small amount of water. Use a whisk to incorporate the butter in small pieces.

🐟 When liquid is blended, remove from heat. Add the orange peels and pecans, and pour over fillets. Serves eight.

Bouquet garni can be made by wrapping cloves, cinnamon and other fragrant spices in a cheesecloth.

189

1801 Post Oak Boulevard Houston, TX 77056 (713) 622-6778

Tony's is an elegant Houston restaurant specializing in French and Mediterranean cuisine. Its three dining rooms feature fresh flowers, art-lined walls, and black-tie European service. The main dining room was described by connoisseur Robert Lawrence Balzer as "one of the most beautiful in America." Tony's is especially proud of its underground wine cellar, containing more than 300 imported wines worth over $800,000.

Owner: Tony Vallone. Reservations suggested. Closed Sunday.

FILLETS OF TROUT WITH TOMATOES AND PESTO SAUCE*

6 fillets of trout	½ cup pesto sauce (recipe
6 ripe tomatoes	below)
Salt and pepper to taste	3 tablespoons butter, cut into
	small pieces

PREPARATION TIME: 15 MINUTES   COOKING TIME: 20—30 MINUTES

▶ Peel, slice and seed tomatoes. Place half the slices in the bottom of a shallow, greased casserole dish. Sprinkle with salt and pepper and bake at 300° F. for 15 minutes.

▶ Place a tablespoon of heated pesto sauce on each fillet, and fold fillet in half over sauce.

▶ Place folded fillets over baked tomato slices. Cover with remaining slices and dot with 3 tablespoons of diced butter. Broil 5 to 10 minutes or until fish flakes when tested with a fork. Can be served hot or cold. Serves six.

*PESTO SAUCE

1 cup coarsely chopped fresh	4 ripe tomatoes, peeled and
basil, moderately packed	seeded
½ cup olive oil	¼ cup pine nuts (available in
Salt and pepper to taste	gourmet shops)
	⅓ cup grated Parmesan cheese

PREPARATION TIME: 15 MINUTES

▶ Combine the ingredients in a blender until fairly smooth.
▶ Heat blended mixture in a saucepan before spooning onto fillets.

567 Hudson Street New York, NY 10014 (212) 243-9260

The White Horse Tavern, one of the best-known taverns in New York, is housed in a building that dates back to 1817. The Greenwich Village Tavern was established in 1880 and was frequented by Welsh poet Dylan Thomas. Its menu is composed of sandwiches, burgers and salads.

Owner: Edward Brennan. Reservations not accepted. Open seven days.

FISH & CHIPS

2 3-oz. scrod fillets	1 tablespoon cornmeal
1 cup flour	Salt and pepper to taste
1 teaspoon baking powder	Beer
½ teaspoon baking soda	Hot french-fried potatoes
1 egg	

PREPARATION TIME: 5 MINUTES   COOKING TIME: 8 MINUTES

▶ Combine flour, baking powder, baking soda, cornmeal, salt, pepper and egg. Mix well, and add as much beer as is necessary for a thick batter.

▶ Dip fish in mixture and deep-fry for approximately 8 minutes or until golden brown. Serve on a bed of french fries. Serves one.

TUNA SALAD

1 lb. tuna packed in water	4 carrots, grated
1 stalk celery, diced	¼ cup fennel seed, ground
2 green peppers, diced	Mayonnaise to taste
2 onions, diced	

▶ Combine all ingredients. Serve on bread or with salad greens. Serves four.

SEAFOOD COOKERY INDEX

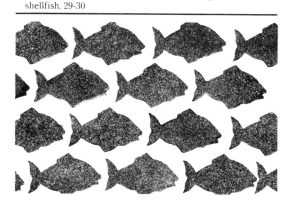